the practical spinner's guide

Silk

Sara Lamb

INTERWEAVE.
interweave.com

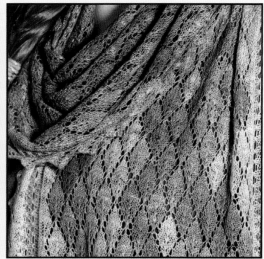

EDITOR
Ann Budd

ASSOCIATE ART DIRECTOR
Julia Boyles

PROJECT & SAMPLE PHOTOGRAPHER
Joe Coca

**PHOTO STYLIST &
STEP-BY-STEP PHOTOGRAPHER**
Ann Swanson

COVER & INTERIOR DESIGN
Adrian Newman

PRODUCTION
Katherine Jackson

Interweave
A division of F+W Media, Inc.
4868 Innovation Drive
Fort Collins, CO 80525
interweave.com

Manufactured in China by RR Donnelley Shenzhen.

Library of Congress Cataloging-in-Publication Data

Lamb, Sara, 1951-

Silk / Sara Lamb.

    pages cm. -- (The practical spinner's guide)

Includes bibliographical references and index.

ISBN 978-1-59668-680-9 (pbk)
ISBN 978-1-62033-472-0 (PDF)

1. Hand spinning. 2. Silk. 3. Yarn. I. Title.

TT847.L359 2014

677'.39--dc23

                                    2013036950

10 9 8 7 6 5 4 3 2 1

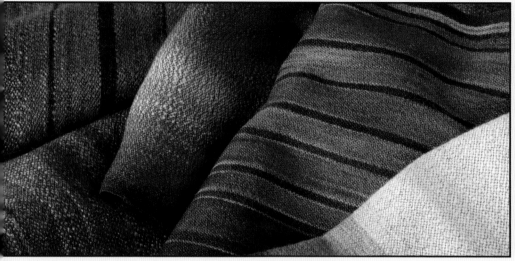

Acknowledgments

'IN MY STUDIO ABOVE MY DESK is a sign that encourages me to keep working, even if it's only a little bit each day: Everything Furthers. Each idea, each word, each project in this book is the result of years of collaboration with many people, some of whom were aware of the collaboration, some of whom were not. Nothing is created alone!

First, thank you, Linda Ligon, founder and creative director at Interweave, for asking me to undertake this project. Linda has been an advocate for textiles and a supportive voice for many years. I appreciate all she has done more than these words can say.

Thank you to Ann Budd, my editor, for her guidance and expert handling throughout the weeks and months of putting this book, our second project, together. Thanks also to Maggie Casey, my technical editor, for her kind oversight as she helped to clarify and correct my words so that the reader wouldn't be confused. Thanks to Ann Swanson once again—her excellent photos make the text come alive and I depend on them for clarification of my often halting and inadequate words. I'm also grateful to the many people who work behind the scenes at Interweave for making this book possible.

I thank my weaving and spinning friends for their help, advice, fiber, as well as for their knitting and weaving skills. In addition, their many hours on the phone or in person helped me puzzle out how and what to say about all of this silk, which is one of my favorite fibers to spin and certainly to wear. I'm grateful also to the vendors and suppliers who provided me with fiber, dyes, tools, and inspiration—may we meet again soon and often!

Thanks once again to my family for putting up with Distracted Me during these months, all the while hoping that the state wasn't permanent. Particular thanks to my husband, Kurt, who listened patiently, offered advice, encouraged me, and remained unfailingly supportive as I spun the silk and text threads that are woven together to create this volume.

TABLE *of* CONTENTS

SILK: *The Luxury Fiber*

IN 1980, I BOUGHT A PORTION OF A TUSSAH silk brick to spin. I was an experienced spinner by then, having spun a lot of wool, some linen, plenty of ramie, and some cotton. I decided that silk was the next fiber to try, and I knew it would be a challenge for me—it's a slick fiber, very fine, and a bit pricey, and I wanted to do it "right."

I saved and admired the fiber for a while, building up my confidence by reading and asking around, finding as much information as I could about spinning silk. The portion of a silk brick that I had was wide and dense, and the fibers I could pull from it were of varying lengths. Spinning from the end of the brick left a mess of disorganized fibers in my hand. Holding tighter to prevent this mess mostly resulted in my fighting the fiber, as I tried to draft one end of fibers that had already been pulled into the yarn at the other end. The process didn't go well, and I ended up with a mass of silk and sweaty palms.

I hunted through books and fiber magazines—there was very little written information available. In *Spinning Wheels: Spinners and Spinning* (see Bibliography), Patricia Baines mentions dividing the thick sliver lengthwise and into small sections, then folding it over a forefinger and spinning from the fold. When I tried this, the silk spun like, well, silk! Cheryl Kolander's *A Silkworker's Notebook* includes a drawing of a hand holding disorganized fibers and drafting a fine silk yarn from them. This image helped solve second part of the puzzle—what to do with the mass of fibers left when the first part of the bundle drafted smoothly!

I wanted to weave my handspun silk into fabric, and I wanted it to look and feel silky, not rough or rustic. I wanted to weave a fabric that would instantly be recognized as "silk." I divided the tussah I had into two lots: 2 ounces (57 grams) for a two-ply warp yarn and 1 ounce (28.5 grams) for a singles weft. I finished both yarns with a wash in hot water and hung them to dry.

The warping, weaving, and finishing of the cloth went quite well. However, the result was not what I had imagined. Although it was silky and soft, the cloth did not shine as I'd expected, and the surface was fuzzier than I wanted. It took a few years for me to discover why and to learn how to produce the cloth I wanted. In these pages, you'll learn what I learned—how I improved my spinning and focused my weaving to finally be able to make the silk fabric I'd envisioned at the beginning.

I spun tussah silk brick for my first woven silk scarf.

A Bit of History

ALTHOUGH THE TRUE ORIGINS of the discovery of silk are lost in time, the fiber and fabric are legendary. They play an important role in commerce, in culture, in fashion, and in the formation of political and economic alliances from before recorded history. The Chinese character for silk has been a part of the written word for thousands of years, and the Roman word for silk, *ser*, has given us our name for the process of raising and cultivating silk—sericulture.

Silk is known the world over as a luxurious smooth, shiny, soft, and insulating fiber. Not only is it prized for its beauty, but also equated with wealth and position, and valued for its rarity. However, the degree to which silk embodies any of these properties varies according to the fiber quality and type and how the silk is produced. For the most part, silk cocoons are raised for reeling, in which several cocoons are unwound into continuous fibers. The leftovers from this process, as well as cocoons too damaged to reel, are available as fiber to handspinners.

For centuries, silk has been used for every precious object imaginable, from bookbinding to papermaking, embroidery, and all types of textiles. Any discussion of silk leads us

According to legend, Lady Xi-Ling, the wife of a long-ago Emperor of China, was taking tea in her garden, when a silk cocoon fell into her hot tea water. She noticed a fine thread unwrapping from the cocoon and realized that "what the worm had wound, could be unwound" into thread for weaving and embroidery.

In another version of this legend, the Emperor's wife watches the worm spin its cocoon in the branches of trees in her garden and imagines that the thread, so expertly wound, could be unwound.

down the paths of history, geography, myth and legend, science, tools and techniques, and the mysteries of dyes and dyeing. In fact, the famed Silk Road was not one path from China to the West, but several routes through Central Asia that varied according to changes in the political climate.

Myths and legends abound about the origin of silk and the discovery of silk as a fiber. Most scholars agree that silk has been used as a fiber and fabric for more than 5,000 years, and perhaps much longer. Fragmentary fabric evidence from both China and India dates to more than 2,000 years B.C. In China, "the Chronicles of Chou-King," dating from 2200 B.C., identifies Shantung as the birthplace of sericulture. In India, the epic *Mahabharata*, which is thought to date as far back as 4000 B.C., mentions a silk woven cloth.

China jealously guarded the secret of sericulture to control the prosperous commodity and exploit it for its trade value. Inevitably, the seeds (eggs of the silkworm) and the secrets of how to cultivate them, were smuggled to

> A Chinese princess, who was about to marry far from home, smuggled a few silkworm eggs into the folds of her headdress, bringing silk cultivation and production to her new home in the fourth century A.D. Although the disclosure of silk-production secrets was harshly punished, the princess and other brave souls successfully established sericulture throughout Asia.

Korea, and from there to Japan, through India to Persia, and farther on to the West.

Some scholars believe that mulberry silk (from the *Bombyx mori* silkworm) developed in China, while, simultaneously, India developed fiber and fabric from the various *sub-Himalayan* wild silks—muga (from the *Antherae assamensis* silkworm), eri (from the *Samia cynthia ricini* silkworm), and tussah, also Tassar, (from the *Antherea mylitta* and *Antheraea proglei* silkworms). No matter where silk originated, or which variety was cultivated where or when, silk itself has played an important role in the development of world commerce, trade, and the spread of civilization.

Silk cultivated in China became an important trade commodity for every country between China and England along the Silk Road. At each stop, the value increased by the surcharge of the new handlers. From the routes that led over the high desert plains from China to Persia (present-day Iran), Persian traders carried the silk farther west through what are now Iraq, Afghanistan, and Turkey. From there, silk fabrics traveled both north to Europe and south into North Africa.

Many attempts were made to break the monopoly of Chinese silk cultivation. Two monks, visiting from the west, smuggled eggs out of Asia (most likely from Khotan) in hollowed-out walking sticks, bringing the precious cargo back to Byzantine Emperor Justinian (circa A.D. 483–565). With the capture and relocation of the best silk weavers, the Emperor re-established cultivation and production of silk fiber for weaving and embroidery, which had been lost to Persia through conquest.

As the result of wars and conflict, many silk workers were captured as slaves so that their skills and tools could be passed on to the conquering countries. The methods of raising the silkworms themselves gradually traveled through conquest, intrigue, and intermarriage—to Korea, Japan, India, and several Himalayan territories, then on to France, North Africa, and Spain, and even to the New World, as Spain and England attempted to establish colonies of silk workers. Brazil continues to be one of the leading producers of raw silk. Over time, skills and knowledge, as well as raw materials, traveled throughout the world, wherever skilled silk workers, weavers, and embroiders happened to land.

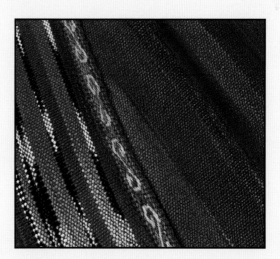

CHAPTER ONE:

Silk Basics

The life cycle of a moth is simple, focused, and predictable. Each adult female fertilized moth lays several hundred eggs. When these hatch, the larva go through at least four stages of eating, growing, molting, and eating again, until the silkworm (technically, it's a caterpillar) reaches its appropriate size, weight, and age. At this point, the silkworm spins the cocoon in which we are all so interested.

A Simple Life

THE NUMBER OF REPRODUCTIVE cycles per annum (called voltinism) in silk moths is directly related to the climate in which they live. Univoltine moths live in climates characterized by cold winters that force hibernation—these moths have a single breeding cycle per year. Bivoltine moths live in the more temperate climates of China, Korea, Japan, and other parts of Asia, and breed twice a year. Polyvoltine moths, raised in warm tropical climates, may breed several times each year. Many attempts are being made to cross various types of moths to increase voltinism and, therefore, garner more silk fiber.

The full-grown silkworm finds (or is provided) a suitable place to attach the cocoon. In captivity, this may be a branch, box, or basket provided by the farmer. In the wild, it's most likely a branch or the crook where a leaf attaches to a branch. Farmers protect the silkworms reared in the wild from predators as best they can, or collect the cocoons and relocate them indoors, or provide a semisecluded indoor space for the worms to spin their cocoons and emerge to mate, lay eggs, and start the cycle again.

If the cocoons are to be reeled, the worms are stifled (euphemism for "killed") before they become moths, and the cocoons are examined and graded, the best to be sent for reeling. The cocoons that are too misshapen or damaged for reeling are put aside as waste to be sent to machines that will break them apart and prepare the fiber into top. This waste silk is the silk we eventually spin.

Varieties of Silk

AT THIS TIME, CHINA PRODUCES more silk than any other country, surpassing even Japan in the late twentieth century. Most of that silk fiber production is from the domesticated *Bombyx mori* silk moth, which produces a pure white lustrous filament. The second most abundant form of silk fiber produced is from the tussah silk moth, also from China. In addition, there are several other varieties of wild silks from India, Southeast Asia, and Africa.

Silk is available in many forms, including cocoons, unprocessed fiber, and yarn.

Cultivated Silk

Bombyx silk, produced by the *Bombyx mori* moth, is the fine, bright white fiber we think of as pure silk. This lustrous and shiny variety accounts for the majority of silk on the commercial market. Bombyx, as it is commonly called, is also known as mulberry silk, because of the silkworms' exclusive diet of mulberry leaves.

Bombyx silkworms are raised on farms, where the farmer provides a secure and predator-free environment for the silkworms to grow, as well as a continuous supply of mulberry leaves. The life cycle of this esteemed silkworm is controlled at every step. The process of raising silk fiber starts with reserving a number of cocoons from the reeling process so that they

Bombyx mori *cocoons and fiber are bright white in color; the very fine fibers measure between 9 and 11 microns in diameter.*

may hatch, mate, and produce eggs for the next crop of silkworms and cocoons.

Bombyx silkworms are fed only mulberry leaves, from white, fruitless black, or fruiting black trees. Of these, white mulberry leaves produce the finest and best-quality fiber, followed by leaves from the fruitless black mulberry, then leaves from the fruiting black trees. Other varieties of mulberry leaves, grown in India and North America as either trees or lower growing bushes, are also fed to silkworms.

As noted, several moths from each batch are allowed to hatch, mate, and lay eggs. The female moths are examined to reduce the possibility of disease in the future crop—misshapen or discolored moths and eggs will be destroyed. Each fertilized female silk moth lays more than three hundred eggs, called "seed," onto a gummy paper provided by the farmer to keep the eggs in place.

The moths are confined during the egg-laying process so that each batch of moths and eggs may be examined under a magnifier and isolated if they're found to contain any type of disease or disability. The eggs are closely monitored until they hatch.

Upon hatching, the tiny worms grow through five stages—called instars—eating twice their weight in leaves and molting between each stage. After the fourth molting, they are placed in baskets or boxes provided by the farmer where they spin their cocoons by extruding fibroin covered by a gluey substance called sericin. The colonies are again housed under controlled conditions to ensure the safety of the cocoons as the worms transform into moths.

About five days after formation, the farmer collects the cocoons and stifles the worms. The timing is critical here—if the worm develops too far into the moth stage, the cocoons may be damaged or stained.

Wild Silk

Wild silkworms, including those we know as tussah silkworms, live less restricted lives. Some varieties are gathered from trees and bushes, then the caterpillar is stifled so that the cocoon remains intact and can be reeled. Other varieties are allowed to hatch, which renders the cocoons unreelable. In some cases, the farmer saves a number of cocoons for the next year's crop and allows the moth to emerge and lay eggs (seed). In other cases, mating and egg laying occur in the wild—the farmers hunt for hatched caterpillars, which they house together for feeding and tending until the cocoons are spun.

Several varieties of wild silk moths feed on a number of different trees and are raised to varying degrees without human intervention. Just like their cultivated bombyx cousins, wild silk moths experience distinct growth phases—egg, larva, pupa, and moth. Farmers or silk producers can control some of these phases: cocoons can be gathered to hatch under controlled conditions away from predators, moths can be coerced to lay eggs in specific areas, and the caterpillars can be fed through their several molting processes so that the cocoons are easily secured. However, other than the country of origin, little information is available to handspinners from suppliers about the conditions under which wild silk fiber is produced and harvested.

Tussah Silk

The largest group of wild silks is from the family *Antheraea*, commonly called tussah, or Tassar, silk. *Antheraea pernyi*, from China, *Antheraea mylitta*, from India, and *Antheraea*

Tussah cocoons are large and darker in color than bombyx; the fibers measure between 20 microns and 30 microns in diameter.

Natural colors in tussah varieties range from very light to dark beige and brown.

yamamai, from Japan, are the most common wild silks. Distributors rarely know the particular variety of tussah silk they receive. Most of the tussah available for spinning comes from China, with a lesser amount from India.

Tussah silk cocoons generally are large, reelable, and are treated in much the same manner as bombyx cocoons.

Depending on the variety of the silk moths and what they ate as worms, tussah fiber is golden or honey in color; but it can have a darker, cinnamon tone, as well. This variety of silk has a larger diameter and a less uniform surface than bombyx. Indentations and irregularities on tussah fibers give the lustrous fibers a more sparkly than shiny appearance.

In China, tussah silk is cultivated. The moths are most likely to eat leaves from a variety of oak trees. The silkworms are bivoltine in most

cases (in some colder climates, they're univoltine), and the first crop each year is the finest and softest.

In India, tussah cultivation remains second to bombyx because of the difficulties in rearing and protecting the silkworms from predators and disease. As farmers take a more active role in production, the conditions are more controlled, and tussah production has increased. The farmers secure cocoons to be raised in open sheds, rather than outdoors on trees, and have developed handling processes that ensure greater productivity and higher-quality fiber.

Other Wild Silk
Muga (*Antheraea assama*)

Muga is the fabled golden silk raised and cultivated in the northeastern Indian state of Assam. For centuries, fabric woven from this silk, prized for its luster and golden color, was reserved for royalty and nobility. Recently, the Indian government has supported an economic development program for rural employment, which includes encouragement and assistance for farmers raising muga silk as fiber and turning it into fabric. This type of silk is increasingly available to spinners, both in laps and as top. Muga takes dye beautifully, with an undertone of its natural golden color.

Some tussah fibers are a natural light honey color.

Commercially bleached tussah can be very light in color.

Tussah fibers that will be dyed are often bleached to a lighter color first.

Muga fibers are more golden in color than tussah.

Laps (muga shown here) are produced in the early stages of processing fibers for spinning. The fibers are less uniform in length than in tops and may have more impurities.

Eri (*Samia cynthia ricini*)

There are two types of eri silkworm, differentiated by color—one white and one red. The caterpillars feed on the castor-oil, or "era," plant in Assam, from which the silkworm derives its name. It comes also from the northeastern part of India. Although attempts have been made to transplant this variety to other parts of the world, they have been unsuccessful so far.

Eri cocoons are elongated and have an opening at one end, which prevents them from being reeled. I've found white eri fiber both in laps and as top, but red eri only as laps. In general, eri fibers feel less smooth (more cottony) than bombyx, and the surface of spun yarn shows less of the luster typically associated with bombyx. Although I haven't found any reports on eri fiber size, to me, the fibers feel finer than bombyx.

Because the moth has escaped and left a hole in the cocoon, eri cocoons are not reelable. The fibers are fine and soft.

Cricula Trifenestrata

Another type of Asian silk comes from the curious many-holed cocoon of the family Saturnidae. The *Cricula trifenestrata* silk moth inhabits India, Sri Lanka, Indonesia, and Myanmar. Because of their lacy and hole-studded nature, these cocoons are not reeled, but only spun. The sericin is gold; however, once removed, the silk is light tan. The fibers are short and spin into a fine yarn. Because of the decorative nature of the cocoon itself, it's often left unspun and used as decoration in clothing and for jewelry.

African Wild Silk

Although bombyx was imported centuries ago and used by Moorish weavers and embroiderers in North Africa, Madagascar, West Africa, and Ethiopia, several varieties of wild silk are indigenous to Africa. Many are considered communal brown silk moths.

Anaphe infracta moths live on tamarind leaves and form communal colonies or clusters of cocoons within a casing. Their fiber is rustic, coarse, and strong and is said to resist dye, but I'm skeptical of this last claim. *Anaphe moloneyi* moths also form clusters of cocoons, but they're not enclosed in a casing. They produce a coarse, rough fiber that is lighter in color than *A. infracta. Gonometra rufobrannea aurivillius* comes from Zimbabwe and is pale gray in color. The sample I have is a loosely combed mass of fibers that seem finer than tussah to my fingers. It spins into a softly lustrous fine yarn.

The red color in red eri silk is produced by sericin, which is removed in the degumming process.

The fibers in this lap preparation are less uniform and contain impurities that the spinner will have to remove.

Cricula cocoons are riddled with small holes. The degummed fibers are short and spin like cotton.

Bombyx (left) appears smooth and shiny while eri (right) appears fuzzy and cottony.

Gonometra rufobrannea aurivillius *is native to the continent of Africa. The fibers spin fine and smooth.*

Properties of Silk

DESPITE THE MANY VARIETIES OF SILK—from cultivated bombyx to the many wild types—and their diverse origins, they hold many properties in common.

APPEARANCE. One of the finest natural fibers, silk has a diameter as small as 9 microns for cultivated bombyx and up to 25 microns for wild varieties. In terms of length, it's the longest natural fiber, with filaments typically 1,000 to 1,300 yards (914 to 1,189 meters) long and reaching up to 3,000 yards (2,743 meters) long. In cross section, the fiber is triangular, which allows it to reflect light with its characteristic shine.

STRENGTH. Silk is known for its strength (but not durability). A cocoon needs to be strong enough to hold the silkworm for the duration of her metamorphosis into a moth. However, the moth has to be able to escape the cocoon once the change has occurred. To do so, she secretes an alkaline substance that dissolves a hole through the cocoon. As a result of this necessary property, silk fibers can be dissolved in a number of chemicals. Alkaline-based liquids or mineral acids will burn holes right through the fibers, while sunlight and even oxygen can degrade them.

MOISTURE ABSORPTION. Silk is able to absorb about 30 percent of its weight in moisture. This greatly aids the fibers in their ability to absorb dyes and makes silk one of the most pleasing fibers to dye. However, silk will also absorb impurities, such as metal salts, which can damage the fibers. "Weighted" silk fibers have been subjected to a process that intentionally adds metal salts to give the fiber a crisper hand but compromises its durability.

ELASTICITY. Silk has good elasticity, but not quite as good as wool. Silk fibers can stretch up to 20 percent when dry and up to 35 percent

One bleached and two natural colors of tussah were used to spin the yarns in this cloth. Although washed before weaving, additional shrinkage occurred in the finishing process, resulting in an undulating edge.

when wet. Dry silk will break when stretched more than 20 percent. Silk's ability to stretch puts it in high demand, especially for such items as parachutes.

HEAT REACTION. At temperatures above about 300°F (150°C), the molecular structure of silk starts to break down and the fiber begins to turn yellowish. To avoid discoloration, it's important to iron silk on a medium heat setting or use a damp pressing cloth between the iron and the fabric. Silk burns with a sputtering flame, leaving a crisp brittle ash and an odor much the same as burnt hair or feathers.

SUSCEPTIBILITIES. Chlorine bleach will dissolve silk. Silk is damaged by perspiration, which will weaken and discolor the fibers. It's also harmed by aluminum chloride, a chemical commonly added to antiperspirants. In addition, ultraviolet rays can destroy silk fibers. As little as six hours of direct exposure may damage the fibers as much as 60 percent. Oxygen is also harmful, and unless kept in sealed containers, silk will eventually break down. Although silk is resistant to mildew and moths, it's vulnerable to carpet beetles.

SHRINKAGE. Silk shrinks with washing; the degree of shrinkage determined by the variety. Take this into account when you combine two or more silks in the same fabric. Some of this shrinkage can be attributed to yarns relaxing during finishing. With forceful pressing and tentering (stretching on a frame), many silk fabrics can regain most of what's lost. However, the restretching process will reduce some of the fabric's elasticity, because the fibers will be stretched to their full extent in the process. Woven fabrics will shrink more in the warp-wise direction, but this shrinkage is also attributable to the weaving process, which keeps these yarns under tension and is accounted for in the take-up measurement when calculating warp lengths.

Fiber Processing

REELED SILK YARNS ARE THE HIGHEST quality silk yarns on the market. The reeling process involves unwinding the silk filament from silkworm cocoons, sometimes several at once, into a continuous thread that's processed for embroidery and weaving. Reeled silk fiber is not used by spinners but, fortunately, the process generates much waste fiber—the beginnings and ends of cocoons and broken, breached, and misshapen ones—that is

Silk fiber is available in many forms, including "top" (left), folded into a "brick" (center), or in "laps" (right).

available for handspinning. This waste fiber is processed into a variety of preparations available to both machine and handspinners: top (also called sliver), bricks, and laps. Each form represents a different stage in the process of fiber preparation for commercial spinning.

In the first step in processing silk for spinning, broken silk cocoons and waste fibers are put through a series of degumming baths consisting of very hot water, detergent or cleaning agent, and an alkaline substance that helps soften and dissolve the sericin.

Next, cocoons are mechanically torn apart and aligned on a large drum cylinder fitted with sharp teeth (similar to carder cloth) until a sufficient quantity is wound onto the cylinder. This preparation, called a lap, is then removed and sent to a machine that further draws out the fibers and cuts them into uniform lengths for further preparation. Filament waste fibers do not need to go through this process.

The aligned fibers are put through a combing process that chops the fibers at random, then sorts and straightens them and removes any remaining bits and pieces of cocoon and other foreign matter. The first pass through the equipment produces Grade A-1 fiber. Many passes through the process may be required before a batch of fiber is completely cleaned and aligned. Each subsequent pass produces sheets of fiber with a shorter and shorter length. The sixth or seventh sheet contains only very short fibers that are considered of lesser grade.

The combed sheets of silk are passed through a series of belts and toothed cloth that attenuate them in to a thin film. The film is then wrapped around a metal core that's pulled through another machine in which the fiber is drawn into top, or sliver, which is the most common preparation available to spinners.

Grades of Silk

The grade of silk fiber (whether bombyx or a wild variety) is based on the quality, length, color, and condition of the fibers used in the preparation. Be aware that not all preparations are labeled and, in these cases, you'll have to trust your fingers, your eyes, and your supplier.

The better silks—A-1 or A grade—will feel soft and silky, not brittle or chalky, and will have staples as long as 5 or 6 inches (12.5 or 15 cm) with only slight variation in fiber length. The fibers will be fine and very smooth, something you'll feel in your fingers as you spin.

Silks of lesser quality, B and C grade, can have a dull appearance, shorter overall staple length, and may contain clumps of short fibers. The fibers will feel less smooth, almost as if they were coated with a powdery substance. I have spun B- and C-grade bombyx tops and, although they make nice fabrics, they look more like cotton than silk—the luster just isn't there. However, these silks cost less and are useful as weft for less fancy cloth or garments.

In addition to grades of silk, tussah tops are available in various shades of natural golden or tan colors, or they may be bleached to a whiter color. Unbleached does not necessarily mean better quality; there are some bleached tussah fibers of quite good quality. Again, your hands and fingers will tell you whether the fiber is sound or damaged and whether it will produce a silky lustrous fabric or an irregular rustic one.

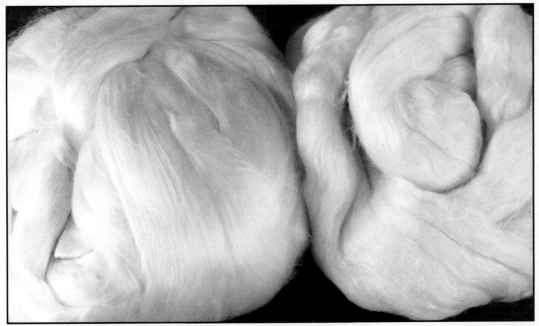

A-grade silk (left) is longer, smoother, and has more luster than C-grade silk (right).

Natural tussah fibers are golden or tan (left), but they can be bleached (right) to enhance dye takeup.

Silk Blends

SILK IS COMMONLY BLENDED with other fibers. Silk adds luster and strength to many soft fibers and durability to blends that contain delicate or fragile fibers.

Some of the most popular blends include animal fibers. I've used blends of silk with merino, Bluefaced Leicester, cashmere, and alpaca in the projects and samples in this book. But be aware that silk can be so strong compared to more delicate fibers, such as cashmere, yak, or bison, that it may visibly abrade those fibers in hard-use or hard-wear areas of a textile. Therefore, these blends are best used for shawls and scarves, where silk's luster and drape will show to full advantage without its strength becoming a hindrance.

Silk is also commonly combined with cotton. Both fibers are slick and fine, and they have similar thermal properties—cool in hot weather and warm in cool weather, at least when dry. Another advantage is that both can be dyed with the same fiber-reactive dyes when used with an alkaline fixative, although silk should always be neutralized with a weak acid solution following any alkaline application. See Chapter 3 for more on dyeing silk.

Many of my fabrics are spun from silk blended with merino, Bluefaced Leicester, cashmere, and alpaca.

In addition to blending fibers before spinning, you can spin the fibers separately, then ply them together. Traditional Orenburg lace shawls, for example, are knitted with yarn comprised of two plies—one ply is fine goat hair and the other is silk. The silk adds drape and weight to the lofty mohair, with exquisite results.

In weaving, silk is strong enough to be used in the warp. Crossed with wool or cotton in the weft, the fabric will drape and breathe. Of course, it's also quite nice to reverse the fibers and use silk in the weft instead. Again, silk is so strong that it might abrade very fine fibers during weaving and wearing, so combinations that involve cashmere, fine bison, or yak might best be limited to loosely worn shawls and scarves instead of tailored garments.

I have seen blends of silk and linen fiber for sale but, as yet, I haven't tried to spin such a blend. It would make nice paper and should make durable, crisp, and shiny fabrics.

Top row, left to right: bombyx silk and yak; bombyx silk and white cashmere; tussah silk and brown cashmere. Bottom row, left to right: bombyx silk and cashmere; cotton and silk; tussah and yak.

Blending Silk

It's easy to make your own silk blends, whether you want to blend silk with other fibers or blend different colors of pure silk.

Blending by Hand

You can blend combed silk in top or brick with another fiber that has also been combed by simply stacking small amounts of the two and pulling by hand along the lengthwise grain of the top. You can repeat the process of stacking and pulling until you get the desired blend. Blend by hand to maintain as much of the alignment in the prepared top as possible while blending colors or fibers.

To blend colors of prepared top by hand, hold small amounts of each color to be blended, pull them, and re-stack them. Spin from this blend for a variegated yarn.

MAINTAINING CONSISTENT PROPORTIONS

When you blend fibers or colors for a large project, you'll want to take care to keep the proportions of each consistent from batch to batch. For example, let's say that we want 16 ounces (454 grams) of a blend that's 80 percent merino and 20 percent silk.

To begin, determine how much you'll need of each fiber by multiplying the percentage of each fiber by the total amount desired.

80% merino × 16 oz (454 g) = 12.8 oz (362.9 g)

20% silk × 16 oz (454 g) = 3.2 oz (90.7 g)

Weigh out the appropriate amounts of each fiber. For the example, weigh 12.8 ounces (362.9 grams) of merino and 3.2 ounces (90.7 grams) of silk.

Because you can only card about ½ ounce (14 grams) of fiber at a time, you need to break down your fiber into smaller units. To maintain consistent proportions, you multiply the percentage of each fiber by ½ ounce (14 grams). At this point, it's easier to work in grams than ounces.

80% merino × 14 g = 11.2 g

20% silk × 14 g = 2.8 g

If your scale doesn't report tenths of grams, you'll need to guesstimate these amounts or weigh larger lots and break them down by eye to the smaller units you need.

Load 11.2 grams of merino and 2.8 grams of silk as evenly as possible on the carder. Card carefully and slowly, watching for damaged fibers, until the two are well-blended. Repeat this step for each 14-gram blend.

When it comes time to spin these blends, take care to hold the carded preparation loosely to allow the fibers to draft as smoothly as possible.

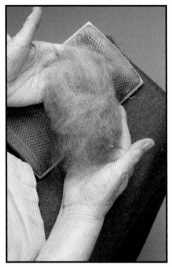

Layer the colors on handcards (or drumcards) in the proportion you want.

Card until the colors are blended to the desired degree.

Remove the fibers and spin from the carded bundle.

Silk noil adds texture to wool yarns: layer the wool and then the silk noils onto the carders.

Card the fibers together to blend.

Spin the textured blend from carded rolags.

Carding

You can also blend fibers by carding, although the carded fibers won't be as organized as those in the original combed preparation. If you use a drumcarder, take care not to overload the carder and remember to rotate it slowly. If you use handcards, use cotton carders, which have finer and more closely spaced teeth than wool carders and which will cause less damage to fine fibers.

In both cases, use small amounts of fiber, work gently and slowly, and watch out for broken and damaged fibers, which will appear as neps or noils. Be aware that silk top and bricks contain fibers of various lengths and shorter fibers can clump together to produce lumps in the carded preparation. You may wish to cut the silk fibers to more closely approximate the staple length of the fibers you card with them.

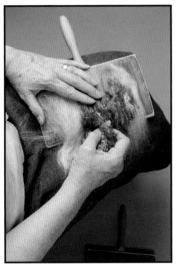

Sari silk threads can be layered with silk top to make a textured yarn.

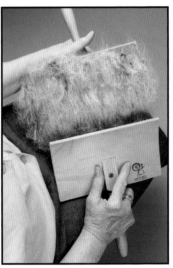

Card the fibers until they're blended as evenly as you like.

Remove the bundle from the carders to spin.

CHAPTER TWO

Spinning Silk

For centuries, silk has been spun on spindles and driven spindles (charkhas) for embroidery and woven fabric. Most sericulture is focused on cocoons that can be reeled. The reeling process produces some waste—cocoons not fit for reeling and disorganized fibers from the beginning or end of the cocoon. This waste fiber can be prepared by hand and spun as a rustic yarn or arranged into a mat or wadding for quilted clothing or bedding.

When demand for silk clothing grew with the rise of the middle class, it became profitable to spin waste silk fiber. Such yarns were labeled "spun silk" to distinguish them from reeled silk. With the advent of the Industrial Revolution, the waste from silk reeling was mechanically processed and turned into a fiber preparation that could be spun by machine—a process called "cottonizing." Thanks to this process, handspinners now have access to a number of varieties of silk top.

Equipment

'YOU DON'T NEED SPECIAL EQUIPMENT to spin silk. What's most important is that the equipment is comfortable for you and produces the results you want. In general, you'll need a wheel or spindle and some means to wind the yarn so that it doesn't tangle and is easy to use for weaving or knitting, as well as for crochet, embroidery, and other needlework.

Spun silk (left) can be smooth and tightly twisted. Reeled silk (right), which is composed of filament strands, is stronger and more lustrous, with or without added twist. Reeled silk by Michael Cook.

Spinning Wheels

Over many years, I've spun silk on a variety of wheels. I don't believe that any drive system is inherently better than another, but you may prefer one to another. I use double-drive and flyer-lead (scotch) tension most often, but my fastest wheel is bobbin-lead (Irish) tension with no tensioning device whatsoever. If I were to choose only one wheel-drive system, it would be flyer-lead, with a separate drive band from the drive wheel to the flyer whorl and a brake band on the bobbin. It's simple to set up, easy to adjust while spinning, and readily available among the wheels manufactured today.

Because I spin fine yarns, whether for weaving or knitting, that require a lot of twist, my quest has always been to find the fastest wheel possible that's easy to set up and use and that isn't easily bumped or displaced out of alignment. I want a wheel that's stable and sturdy, not wobbly or warped in any way. I also prefer a wheel for which additional parts (such as bobbins or whorls) can be obtained and one that can be serviced by its maker.

I've not found an antique wheel that meets all of these requirements, but several contemporary ones do. I encourage you to find a solid wheel made by a reputable maker in your country. Find a maker who understands spinning in addition to woodworking—both are key to a good wheel. Ideally, choose a wheel made from hardwood, such as maple, walnut, or cherry, that will withstand years of repetitive motion without parts wiggling out of place.

In terms of ergonomics, your spinning wheel should be the right height so you don't reach up or down unnecessarily, and it should fit in the space you have available. There's no point in buying a big drive wheel that takes up the entire living room unless you don't plan to use that room for anything else. Upright wheels and wheels with a secondary (accelerator) drive wheel are ideal for small spaces, and they can be made to spin at very high speeds.

Just as people are different, their wheel preferences vary. I've spun on friends' wheels and they on mine. Wheels with fine reputations have not made me happy, and my preferred wheel has frustrated some of my friends. Try out as many wheels as possible before choosing one. Keep in mind that you may need to spin on a wheel for an hour or two before you'll know if it's right for you. Over the years, I've outgrown some wheels as my preferences or my space changed. Luckily, there's a ready market for used wheels, and you can sell one that no longer works for you and buy something else to fit your changing needs.

Spindles

Spindles are an excellent portable choice for spinning silk. For silk, I prefer spindles that weigh about an ounce (28 grams), can hold about half an ounce (14 grams) of yarn, will spin long and fast, and are equally pretty and easy to use!

Like wheels, spindles vary: top-whorl, bottom-whorl, Turkish, supported, mid-whorl, and wheel-driven. All are readily available worldwide from a number of spindle makers and all are appropriate for spinning silk. If you're just beginning, pick up a spindle that's not too heavy, catch some fiber on the hook, and give it a try.

Yarn Winders

Once you've spun your yarn, you'll need to remove it from the bobbin or spindle. To save time and frustration, invest in a tool that can help you do so without causing tangles.

Niddy-Noddies and Skein Winders

Wind yarn directly from your bobbin or spindle onto a niddy-noddy or skein winder. Once the ends have been secured and ties added to hold the strands in place, the skeins are ready to be washed.

Yarn Blocker or PVC Niddy-Noddy

If you want your washed yarn to dry as straight as possible, wind it on a yarn blocker or PVC niddy-noddy. Be careful to wind silk with very slight tension so that you don't inadvertently stretch the yarn—wind just tightly enough to remove the slack. You can also use either of these tools to wind yarns that have been treated with a sizing solution.

Nøstepinnes and Ball Winders

Nøstepinnes and ball winders are handy tools that make easy work of winding yarn into a plying ball. As you wind straight from the skein, spindle, or bobbin, both tools can make two-strand or three-strand balls suitable for plying without adding any twist in the process. This capability lets you have complete control over the twist when plying. Both tools also make nice compact balls ready to be used as warp or weft, or in knitting, embroidery, or needlework.

Keep in mind that silk yarn is slick and slippery to work with and that fibrillates (those fuzzy ends that stick up) may catch on one another and create a sticky mess if not controlled. I like to keep silk yarn under tension whenever possible, and I prefer to pull from the outside of a center-pull ball instead of from the center, which lets the ball eventually collapse on itself. It's a good idea to wind silk yarn around some type of core—a ball of felt, stick of wood, or roll of paper or cardboard—to help keep the yarn in order. Place the wound ball in a small bag or surround it with a "cozy" piece of tubular nylon to control slippage.

Silk Spinning Basics

BEFORE YOU BEGIN TO SPIN, whether you plan to use a wheel or spindle, lay the fiber out on a clean surface and check it for fiber orientation, fiber length, cleanliness, and foreign matter. In general, bricks and top will be smoother than laps. But all preparations, even commercial ones, are likely to contain short fibers and foreign matter that you'll need to pull out as you spin for the smoothest yarn. If your preparation contains a lot of foreign matter, you can expect it to be more difficult to draft, and you're more likely to end up with a textured yarn.

Next, gently pull out a few fibers from the end of the preparation and check for staple length. Check in more than one place to determine whether the staple length is uniform or varies. Bricks and tops, although well-combed and smooth, are still likely to contain fibers of varying length. The average staple length will determine how close, or how far apart, your hands will need to be as you draft new yarn.

To some extent, the preparation will determine the type of yarn that can be spun. Occasionally, even prepared silk fiber can be full of inclusions—chaff, bits of string, and vegetable matter—and I generally want as little of this as possible in my yarn. If the entire preparation has a lot of short bits and chaff, I'll resign myself to a textured, rather than smooth, yarn.

Even well-prepared top may contain short fibers and small bits of foreign matter that will hinder smooth yarn formation.

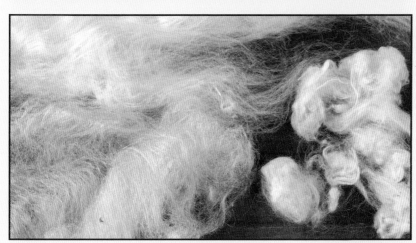

As I spun the commercially prepared eri lap (left), I pulled out short fibers and foreign matter (right).

I spun this textured yarn from muga laps that contained a lot of foreign matter.

Spinning on a Wheel

Before we begin, I want to point out that there's no universally "correct" way to spin. We all develop positions and methods that are most comfortable for our tools, our chairs, and our bodies. Either hand can be forward (closest to the orifice). I'm right-handed, but I like to use my left as the forward hand. I hold the fiber in my right hand, which also controls the drafting zone, something I consider to be key in spinning a uniform yarn. Consequently, I'm most comfortable with a left-flyer spinning wheel or an upright wheel with no orientation to the flyer. These setups let me draft from left to right across my body. If you prefer to use your right hand as the forward hand, an up-right flyer wheel or a right-flyer spinning wheel might be more comfortable for you and allow you to spin without twisting your body.

I spin with my forward hand (the hand toward the orifice) as open as possible. I try not to pinch the yarn, but if I need to retard the twist insertion, I hold the yarn against my open palm and move my hand toward me to increase the pressure. If I tried to pinch the twist instead, my hand and fingers would soon cramp.

CONTROLLING TWIST

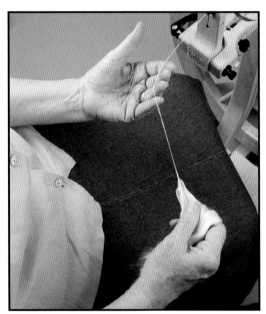

I control the twist insertion with pressure from my open hand.

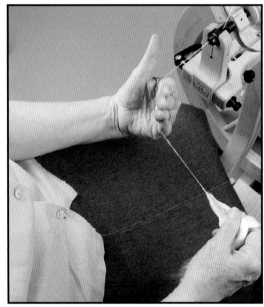

To slow the twist insertion, I pull my forward hand toward me for increased pressure on the fiber.

I typically spin yarn that's small in diameter and, if I pinch the twist, my hands will begin to ache and may suffer permanent damage over time. However, there are times when I do pinch off the twist, or pinch with my fingers to remove chaff or short fibers from the forming yarn. If my pinching fingers begin to ache, I either stop for the day or pay attention to my hand movements to ensure I don't aggravate the discomfort.

I hold the fiber loosely in my other hand as I watch the yarn form at the drafting zone. For me, "loose" is a key word. I start by loosely holding a loose bundle of fibers, and I control the amount of fiber that enters the drafting zone with loose pressure on the bundle.

To spin, I draft a length of yarn, then turn my fiber hand slightly so that my thumb retards the twist. Doing so prevents the emerging twist from drawing in new fiber and gives me time to attenuate the forming yarn until it's stable.

If the preparation is smooth and regular, I'll start with the bundle of fiber folded over my index finger. As the fiber is drafted out and the bundle gets smaller, I'll transfer the bundle to the palm of my hand and keep drafting from the folded fibers until all the fibers are incorporated into the yarn. Because silk is a slick fiber, it drafts out easily if the fibers are held loosely, and the twist doesn't enter the fiber past the drafting zone. Even the disordered mass at the end of the bundle will draft out a fine yarn if held softly but firmly.

I like to use both hands equally when I spin. First, I draft backward with my fiber hand, then I hold the fiber steady as I draft forward with my forward hand. I alternate so that both hands are moving and changing position and there's less chance of repetitive-motion injury.

DEALING WITH SLUBS

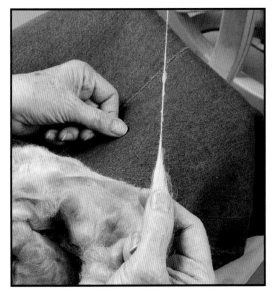

A slub of short fibers or foreign material will sit on the surface of the yarn.

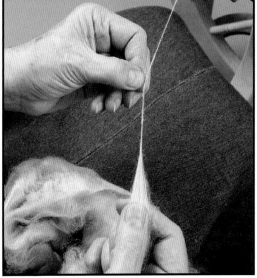

To remove a slub, slow down your treadling to reduce twist buildup as you pinch off the slub.

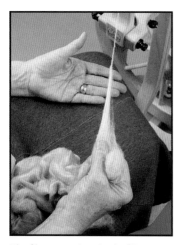

The fibers entering the drafting zone should be mostly aligned and free of foreign material.

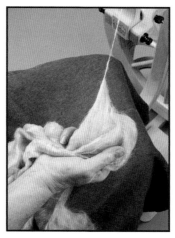

Even if the fiber bundle is disorganized in your hand, silk will draft out mostly aligned with the spun yarn.

Draft out the fiber and continue to attenuate (stretch) the yarn until it will stretch no more.

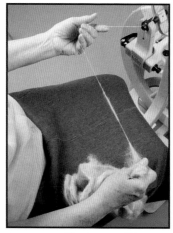

Lumps caused by clumps of fibers can be attenuated as you continue to insert twist.

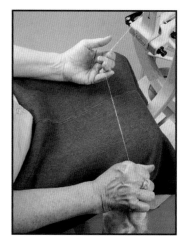

To attenuate the yarn, turn your fiber hand to stop twist from drawing new fibers and gently stretch the yarn between your hands as the lump is stretched and stabilized with new twist.

DRAFTING FROM THE FOLD

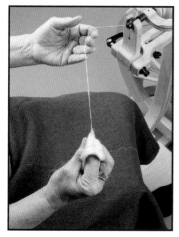

Fiber can be drafted from the folded bundle of silk held over your index finger.

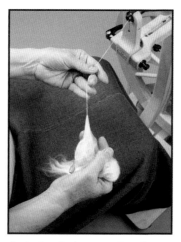

As the bundle decreases, transfer the fiber to your palm and continue drafting from the fold.

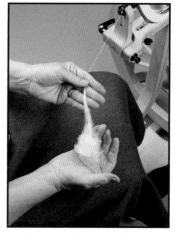

Continue to pull out a uniform amount of fiber from the disordered mass at the end of the bundle.

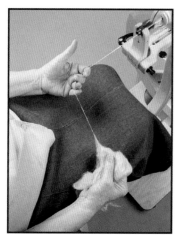

I use my fiber hand to draft away from my forward hand.

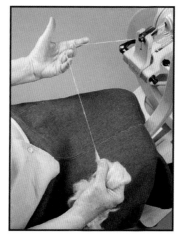

Then, I hold my fiber hand steady as I use my forward hand to draft fibers out of the bundle.

Spinning on a Top-Whorl Spindle

As with wheel spinning, pay attention to the drafting zone and control the orientation and number of fibers drawn in as you spin. In general, I spin the same on top-whorl and supported spindles.

To begin, set the spindle in motion, then move your free hand up to the twist-to-new-fiber contact at the bottom of the drafting zone.

Slightly untwist as you grasp new fiber to prevent the twist from entering the drafting zone.

Continue to draft up and away from the spindle.

Set the spindle in motion, then move your hand up the forming yarn.

Move your free hand up to the drafting zone.

Slightly untwist as you you grasp new fiber.

Spinning Different Preparations

I'VE FOUND THAT THE DIFFERENT preparations of silk require slight differences in the spinning process. In this section, I'll outline the process I use for several types of preparations available to spinners.

Top

Top is the most refined of the silk preparations we can spin, whether it's cultivated or wild silk in origin. It's the final form before machine spinning, and it has a smooth, uniform appearance. Be aware that any grade of silk may be sold as top, so although the preparation is as smooth as the fiber can be made mechanically, the grade of the fiber will still determine the luster and quality of the yarn that can be spun from it. Even top can contain chaff, threads, strings, and bits not removed during fiber processing, so some hand picking might be necessary as you spin.

During mechanical spinning, top is wound through a series of rollers that move at different speeds to attenuate it further. This process allows the machinery to spin a smooth uniform yarn from the end of the top. Although this method works well for mechanical spinning, I find it easier to spin from the fold when handspinning silk top.

Spinning Top or Brick from the Fold

Top and bricks are spun in the same way. To begin, break a small amount of top or brick from the continuous preparation and open it gently by pulling on both ends with your hands.

Fold this fiber over the index finger of your drafting hand and feed the folded fiber into the drafting zone.

Insert twist while you draft back, keeping an eye on the drafting zone—the point at which the fibers turns into yarn. Take care that a uniform amount of fiber is drawn into the yarn and that the fibers are mostly aligned as they feed into the yarn.

"Spinning from the fold" does not have to be over the tip of your finger: the folded fibers may be held in the hand and drafted from the fold without issue. Again, be sure to keep an eye on the drafting zone and take care that a uniform amount of fiber is drawn into the yarn.

As the fiber source diminishes, the folded fiber will turn into a bundle in your hand. Although the final bits will appear to be a tangled mess, they will draft out easily if you hold them loosely in a dry hand. For smooth yarn, make sure that the fibers entering the drafting zone are primarily parallel.

As the yarn is made, there may be lumps of fiber where the twist has jumped past to areas of finer yarn. Attenuate these areas by retarding the twist while continuing to draft back, then insert enough twist to ensure stability of the finished yarn.

Keep in mind that a brick is a distinct form of prepared fiber that's tucked and folded into a compact package. Because top is prepared from bricks, you can expect less uniform fiber length and more extraneous material in bricks than in the more processed top form. Once opened, brick fibers lie mostly parallel, but the preparation is wider and usually denser than top. But, fibers draft easily from this type of preparation.

Laps

Laps are loosely carded/combed fibers in batt-like form. Laps include the fibers that remain on the mechanical carders after the first tearing apart and opening of the waste cocoon. These preparations contain semiparallel fibers and often include a lot of small foreign bodies and other inclusions—bits of cocoon and vegetable matter, stiff and soft threads, and clumps of short fibers, nepps, or noils. Laps are typically further processed into bricks or top.

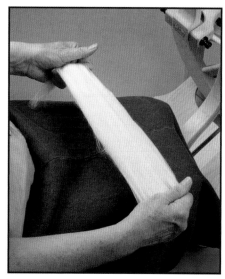

Gently pull the fiber bundle until the fibers begin to slip and loosen the compacted fibers for drafting.

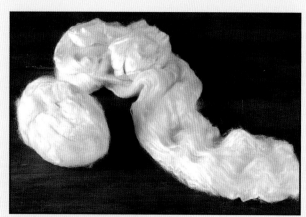

A compact brick of silk (left) and an opened brick of dense, mostly parallel fiber (right).

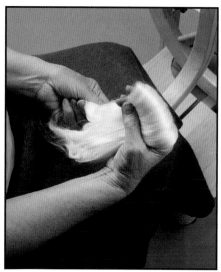

Fold the fiber bundle over the index finger of your fiber hand.

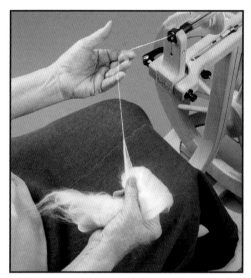

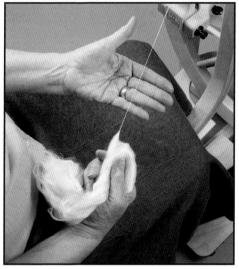

Insert twist as you draft back, keeping an eye on the drafting zone to ensure a uniform amount of fiber is drawn into the yarn.

If you'd rather, you can hold the folded bundle in your hand instead of over the tip of your finger.

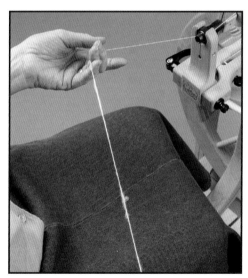

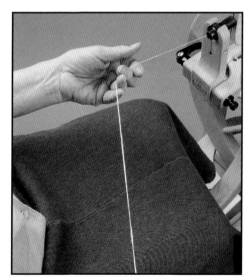

Attenuate lumps by retarding the twist while drafting back.

Allow the twist to enter the attenuated fibers.

Spinning from a Lap

To begin, pull off a bundle of fibers.

Hold the bundle very loosely in your fiber hand and draft directly from the bundle.

As you draft, allow the twist to catch new fibers and help pull them into alignment.

Retard the twist with your forward hand and draft comfortably without twisting your body. Be sure to keep the drafting area stable and watch for clumps and thin areas.

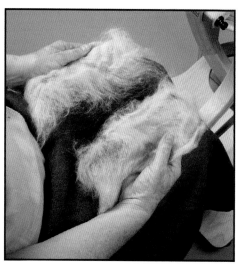

Pull a small amount from the lap.

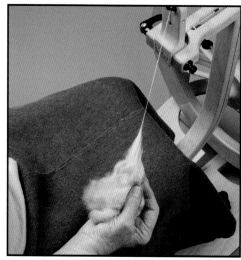

Hold the fibers loosely as the twist pulls them into the forming yarn.

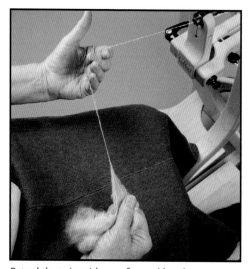

Retard the twist with your forward hand.

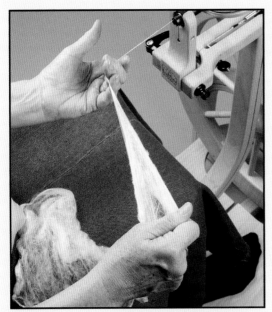

Pull a layer (one attenuated cocoon) from the cap or hankie. The finer the layer, the easier it will be to draft. The drafting zone will elongate as you stretch the hankie and add twist.

Hankies (Mawatas), Bells, and Caps

Some cocoons cannot be reeled, either because the silk moth has broken out, leaving a hole, or because the construction of the cocoon isn't solid. The fiber from these cocoons can be used for an insulating layer in clothing or attenuated to spin into a rustic, more textured, sort of yarn.

Hankies, also called mawatas, are made by wetting and treating any type of cocoon to remove the sericin. The softened cocoons are then gently but firmly pulled onto a frame. (You can make a simple frame with four canvas stretcher bars and four nails.)

Layer several cocoons, one on top of another until a sufficient number is achieved. Leave them to dry on the frame.

Bells and caps are also attenuated cocoons, but are stretched over a form (instead of across a frame) to make a bell-shaped cap of many layers.

Yarn spun from hankies has a textured quality.

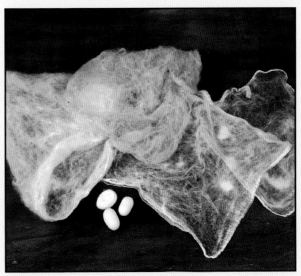

Cocoons, hankies, and bells can be made from any type of silk. Bombyx and tussah are the most common.

Make Your Own Hankie

Any type of cocoon can be made into a hankie, or mawata, at home. The process involves soaking about ten cocoons in hot soapy water, to which a small amount of washing soda (sodium carbonate) has been added—I add ½ teaspoon (2.5 milliliters) of dish detergent and 1 teaspoon (5 milliliters) of washing soda to each gallon (4.5 liters) of water.

To soften the cocoons and remove the sericin coating the fibers, heat them to boiling in the soap-washing soda-water mixture in a Crock-Pot or on the stove. Turn down the heat and simmer for about thirty minutes, then drain and rinse in warm water until the cocoons are cool enough to handle.

While the cocoons are soaking, make a frame out of four sections of artist canvas stretcher boards. Secure each corner with a finishing nail, which will hold the stretched fiber on the frame.

Remove a cocoon and make a hole to begin to attenuate the cocoon, then stretch the fibers with your fingers.

Continue to pull until you can place the stretched edge on two corners of the frame.

Gently pull until all four corners are attached to the frame.

Add layers as desired—the number of cocoons that will fit on a frame depends on the length of the nail.

Repeat the process until all of your cocoons have been attenuated.

When dry, remove the layers from the frame and spin as usual. The eri cocoons shown here are triangular and contain no moth or worm.

Use your fingers to break through softened cocoons and stretch the fibers onto a frame, one layer at a time.

Let the hankies dry, then remove them from the frame and spin as usual.

Spinning from a Hankie, Bell, or Cap

There are two basic ways to spin a hankie, bell, or cap. You can attenuate a single sheet into a long strand and spin from the corner, or you can poke a hold in the center and pull the sheet into a larger and larger ring that you eventually break into a long thin strand. The first method results in a longer drafting zone.

Although a spindle is shown here, the process is the same whether you use a spindle or wheel.

To spin from the corner, separate a single layer from the stack, then pull on a corner to stretch it into a long strand as you draft. As you spin, the drafting zone will be quite long as your fiber hand pulls new fiber from the hankie.

Separate a single layer.

Stretch the layer slightly.

Use your fiber hand to stretch out new fiber from the hankie.

To spin from a ring, separate a single layer, then poke your fingers through the center to make a hole. Pull evenly on all sides of the hole to gradually stretch and attenuate the ring bigger and thinner. Finally, break the ring to make a length of unspun fiber. Attach the fiber to a leader and continue to attenuate as you spin.

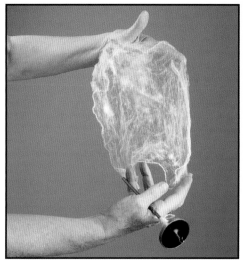
Separate a single layer.

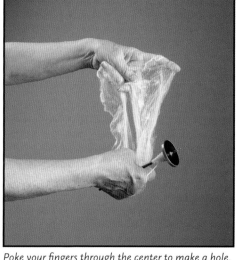
Poke your fingers through the center to make a hole.

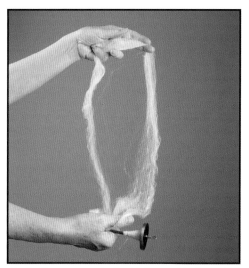
Gradually attenuate the hankie into a thin, large ring.

Break the ring to make a length of unspun fiber.

Other Preparations

Silk is also available in other forms that, because the fibers are short or damaged, are less attractive to handspinners. Silk waste comes in a variety of fibers that will make textured, less lustrous yarns.

Silk waste threads are the waste from the weaving process or threads garnered from pieces of fabric. They are often sold as "sari silk" and come in a variety of lengths and colors. They can be spun into a yarn by themselves or carded with other fibers as accents.

Carrier rods are thick masses of silk fibers that have escaped during the mechanical process of preparing cocoons into sliver and top. The fibers wrap themselves around parts of the machinery and need to be cut off for the machines to continue to operate. The silk mass is removed from the machinery and sold as is.

The fiber can be degummed, dyed, and pulled apart to form a mass of very short fibers for blending or spinning, as you would cotton. This type of silk is often used for embellishment accents or embroidery.

Throwster silk is composed of reeled silk waste threads in a variety of lengths.

Noil comes in the form of batts, top, or loose fibers. Noil is the waste of the waste—the very shortest and most damaged of silk fibers. It must be spun like cotton, with a lot of twist to hold the short fibers together. Noil is blended with other fibers to create texture, and, if dyed, to add color. It spins into a textured yarn; as singles or plied yarn, it makes a wonderful weft for nubby fabrics.

Bottom row (left to right): Silk thread waste; carrier rods; waste. Top row (left to right): Silk noil top and silk noil carded fiber.

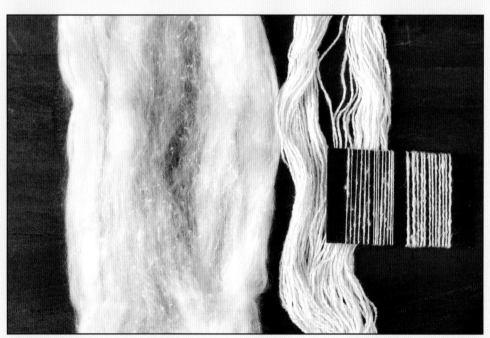

In noil top (left), the fibers are aligned, but they contain small neps or noils, which show up in the yarn as bumps of texture (center and right).

Plying

THERE ARE MANY REASONS to ply yarn. It evens out inconsistencies and orients the fibers to be more parallel with the yarn orientation. It adds strength and increases resistance to abrasion. It also lets you increase the size of your yarn by joining multiple singles without the potential compromise to durability that you risk by spinning heavier grist singles. In addition, plying relaxes the twist inherent in singles, and it allows for specialty effects, such as spiral yarn that results from plying together two weights or two colors of yarn.

Because the twist energy that's inherent in singles can be relaxed in a plied yarn, plied yarns are less lively, more relaxed, and easier to handle. During the finishing process, some singles will mold and bend in their direction of twist, bedding together with their neighbors to give a lively and cohesive surface to woven, as well as knitted fabrics.

Although I can't see the twist angle in a fine white silk yarn as I spin it, I can see the reverse twist build up as I ply. I try to make each length of plied yarn look like a string of beads. As the plied yarn is removed from the bobbin and made into a skein, it may seem very lively and full of twist, but a simple bath will relax the yarn and make it easy to handle for weaving, knitting, crocheting, and other applications.

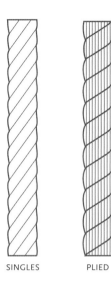

SINGLES PLIED

In a singles yarn, all fibers are twisted together in the same direction. In plied yarns, the fibers are twisted first in the direction of the singles, then in the direction of the ply. They can end up parallel to the strand itself.

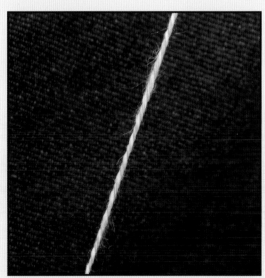

With enough plying twist, the plied yarn resembles a string of beads.

When plying, many spinners advocate winding yarn onto storage bobbins, both to even out areas of uneven twist and to ensure that they're always working with the yarn in the same direction, whether inserting the initial twist or eventual ply into the yarn. To use this technique, place your spindle or bobbin on a lazy kate or in a basket or box where it will unroll freely. Attach the end of the yarn coming off the bobbin to a ball winder, spool, or skein winder. Then, ply these singles from the remaining ends, running them through the plying process in the same direction as the original spinning, or twist insertion.

However, when I wheel spin, I usually ply directly from the bobbin. My bobbins hold a prodigious amount of yarn that represents many hours of spinning over several weeks, and I have found no reason to spend time repackaging this yarn for plying. Because I typically use my handspun yarn for weaving, the yarn I eventually use won't end up in a single orientation anyway. The warp yarns pass back and forth across a warping board, and the weft yarn passes back and forth as the cloth is woven.

Through my experiments with stripes of wool yarn in a single warp, I've found no discernible difference in woven fabric in which the yarns were plied from repackaging, plied from both ends of one ball, or plied from the bobbins on which they were spun. The surface of the fabric and how it behaved during finishing was all the same to my eye and hand. You can find my experiments in *Spin to Weave* (Interweave, 2013), but you may wish to repackage some of your own yarns and test this for yourself.

Keep in mind that when weaving on a loom with a sectional warp beam, which holds the yarn in a single orientation, you may want to work with the yarn in the same direction in which it was spun. It's always a good idea to sample first to see if this might affect your fabric.

For spindle spinning, however, I do repackage the yarns from two or three spindles into a plying ball. Doing so gives me greater control over the spindles as they unwind, removes the plying part from the unwinding part of the process, and gives me a neat package from which to ply.

Wind yarn from two spindles onto a nøstepinne to make a plying ball.

Ply the two yarns together on a plying spindle.

How to Ply

Whether your yarn has been repackaged onto a bobbin, spool, or plying ball, or you plan to ply directly from the spinning wheel bobbin on which it was spun, the method for plying is the same. There are differences, however, in plying on a wheel and on a spindle.

Plying with a Wheel

To begin, tie the singles to the leader with an overhand knot. Hold the twist coming from the spindle or wheel at bay with the hand closest to the orifice or spindle.

Extend the desired number (two, three, or four) singles from the yarn package, keeping them separated by your fingers or the holes in a large button.

Let the twist enter the extended singles, allowing it to build up the desired amount. When there's enough twist in the ply, move your forward hand back to your fiber hand and pinch the twist.

Allow the plied yarn to wind onto the bobbin, retard the twist with your forward hand, and extend a new section for plying.

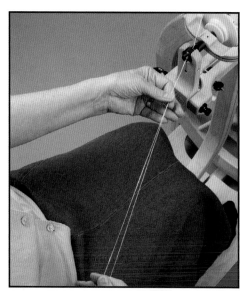

Separate the singles with your fiber hand and hold the twist with your forward hand.

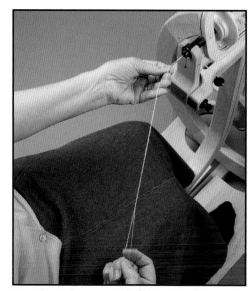

Keep the singles separated while twist builds up.

54

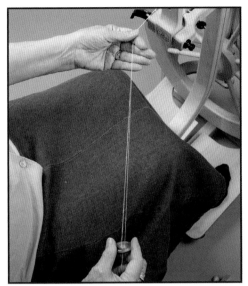

To protect your fingers from abrasion, use a button to separate the plies.

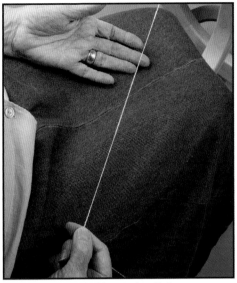

Allow the twist to build up in the plied yarn.

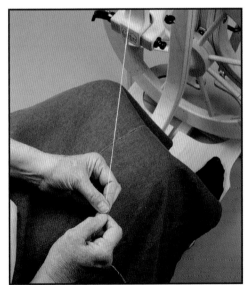

Move your forward hand back to your fiber hand and pinch the twist.

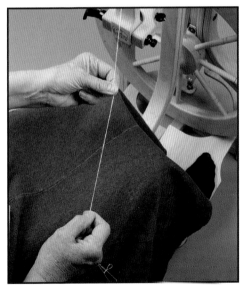

Hold the yarn in your forward hand and allow it to feed onto the bobbin.

Plying with a Spindle

To attach the singles to the spindle, tie the singles into an overhand knot and put the hook between the two strands.

Extend a length of paired singles, then insert twist. Insert plying twist by reversing the spindle direction—clockwise-spun singles will be plied with a counterclockwise twist; counterclockwise-spun singles will be plied with a clockwise twist.

Capture the plied yarn between your fingers to control the twist, then wind the newly plied yarn firmly onto the spindle shaft.

Hook the spindle on the knot between the two singles.

Extend a length, then insert twist.

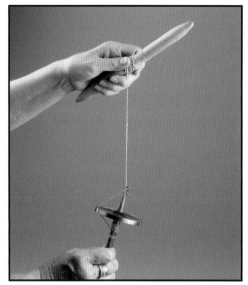

Insert plying twist by reversing the spindle direction.

Capture the plied yarn between your fingers.

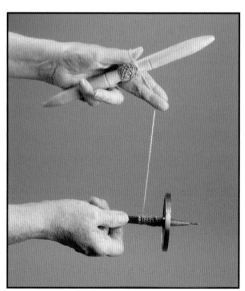

Wind the yarn firmly onto the spindle shaft.

Finishing the Yarn

YARN GENERALLY ISN'T FINISHED until it's been degummed, washed, and hung to dry. These processes remove any remaining sericin, help distribute the twist evenly, and set that twist in the yarn. Silk yarns, whether singles or plied, relax in the finishing process and become easier to manage.

If you wish to dye silk yarn, I recommend degumming it before you dye it. Just like silk fiber, sericin is a protein substance and, as such, dye will affix to it. If you wait to degum until after you've dyed the yarn, some of the dye will wash away with the sericin, and you may be left with a color surprise.

How to Degum Silk

There are a number of ways to degum silk yarn. I've outlined my preferred method for 100 grams of fiber here.

Place the yarn into very hot water with a small amount of detergent (I use hand-dishwashing detergent) and allow it to soak for at least an hour to ensure that it's thoroughly wet.

Prepare a bath of 1 gallon (3.8 liters) of water, ¼ teaspoon (1 milliliter) each of washing soda (sodium carbonate) and detergent (I use dish soap, but any soap formulated to scour fiber is suitable) in a Crock-Pot or nonreactive pot for the stove or oven.

Add the wetted silk to the bath. If you use a pot on the stove, bring the pot to a simmer, then simmer for one hour. If you're using a Crock-Pot, in which the temperature is slow to rise, allow three hours from beginning to end. In you're using an oven, "cook" it at 250°F (121°C) for an hour.

The dissolved sericin will turn the water the color of tea.

Because washing soda (sodium carbonate) is an alkaline substance, it's able to dissolve sericin. But alkaline substances will damage silk if left on the fiber, and heat will accelerate the damage. So be sure to rinse the yarn immediately after degumming and then soak the skein in clear water, to which a mild acid (white vinegar or citric acid) has been added. I add about ½ cup (120 milliliters) vinegar to a gallon (3.8 liters) of warm water for this step, soak the yarn until it's cool, then rinse and dry as usual.

Before washing, wind the yarn into skeins or wind the warp as desired. Place the bobbin, spindle, or ball of yarn a good distance from the niddy-noddy, skein winder, or warping board so that the twist can equalize between areas of very tight twist and areas of less twist as the yarn is wound on. Some spinners do this as a matter of course, either before or after plying.

Secure the yarn with ties in at least four places. Figure-eight ties will help keep the yarn in order during washing and dyeing, and they'll let you easily find the skein structure again after handling. For a warp, tie each section of the cross with figure-eight ties, tie each end, and work the length into a simple crochet chain.

Submerge the skein or warp chain in hot water, along with about ½ teaspoon (2 milliliters) of detergent or a squirt of hand-dishwashing liquid. Let it soak at least an hour (preferably overnight) to fully absorb the water. If you don't have time to wait, cover the yarn with water in a Crock-Pot set on high for a few hours, or cover it with water in a nonreactive pot on the stove over very low heat or in the oven at 200°F (93°C) for at least twenty minutes.

Rinse the yarn in hot water until the water runs clear, squeeze out the excess water, snap the skeins to open and straighten the yarn, and hang to dry.

If the yarn will be knitted, I hang it without weights on a thick rod to dry. If I plan to use singles yarn for weaving, I may block the yarn by rewinding it (with just enough tension to keep it straight and even) on a reel, PVC niddy-noddy, or yarn blocker. If the yarn is blocked under very little, but even, tension, it will bloom and full beautifully when the woven fabric is finished.

Because silk yarn can be very slippery, I prefer to store it in skeins. When beginning a project, I wind the yarn firmly into balls, perhaps

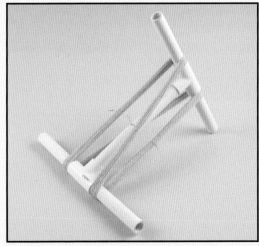

Using very even, slight tension, carefully wind the damp yarn onto a niddy-noddy made from PVC pipe held together with t-joints, and allow it to air-dry.

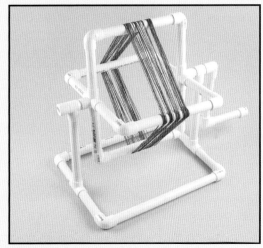

Block larger amounts of yarn on a PVC yarn blocker (see page 134 for details for making your own).

around some type of core, and I secure the ends. If you pull a center-pull ball from the center, the remaining silk will collapse on itself. Instead, use a core to hold the yarn under tension and unwind from the outer edge of the ball.

Dyeing Silk

3

Every form of silk—fiber, yarn, and fabric—takes commercial and natural dyes beautifully. You can easily dye silk at home with acid or fiber-reactive dyes.

However you decide to dye your fiber or yarn, be aware that silk requires more dye per ounce of fiber than other fibers.

For even distribution of color (called level dyeing), the fibers should be thoroughly wetted. Place the silk in a tub of very hot water to which a small amount of hand-dishwashing detergent or other wetting agent (such as Synthrapol) has been added and let it soak overnight. If a long soak time isn't possible, place the silk in a large pot, cover it with enough wetting agent to allow freedom of movement, and let it simmer at about 200°F (93°C) for at least an hour.

Interesting layered effects can occur if the fiber isn't thoroughly wetted. Immersion in low water levels or direct application of dyes to yarn or fiber can create the type of variegation and variations in color depth that are unique to hand-dyed fiber.

Don't be afraid to do your own dyeing. It's easy and safe as long as you follow safety precautions provided by the manufacturers and suppliers, and you're diligent about cleaning your dye area thoroughly after use. Keep in mind that you should never cook with containers or utensils that have been used for dyeing.

Silk can be dyed as fiber or hankies before spinning or as yarn after spinning. You can achieve delightful depth and color variations by blending (by hand or carder) two or more colors together.

You can also choose dyed fibers to complement each other in a plied yarn. For example, ply a solid or semi-solid singles with a variegated singles to emphasize the color changes in the variegated yarn.

Abby Franquemont carded an assortment of dyed fibers to get the depth and color variation in these samples.

If you dye top in a gradual gradient along the length, you can get a pleasing gradient of colors in the spun yarn.

Working with Different Dyes

COMNTEMPORARY COMMERCIAL dyes require three basic elements for success: a proper fixative, enough time to attach to the fibers, and the correct temperature. The type of fixative depends on the type of dye. A dilute organic acid, such as citric acid or acetic acid (household distilled white vinegar), is used with acid-based dyes. An alkaline fixative, such as sodium carbonate (washing soda or soda ash), is used with reactive dyes. Alum (generally in the form of potassium aluminum sulfate), the least toxic of the metal compounds used to fix dyes to fiber (mordants), is used with natural dyes.

The process for applying dyes varies according to the dye type. The methods below outline the way that I use the different types of dyes; other methods will also give good results.

Acid Dyes

Acid dyes are typically used on protein (animal) fibers. These dyes react under acidic (pH 0 to 7) conditions. Although mineral acids (sulfuric, hydrochloric, and boric acids) degrade and dissolve silk, organic acids—such as those used by home dyers—are safe for silk fibers.

I typically use acid dyes for painting fiber or yarn.

To begin, place the wet silk in a bucket and cover it with a 2 percent solution of organic acid (I use citric or acetic acid, or white distilled household vinegar).

CITRIC ACID: Citric acid is available in crystal form wherever dye or soapmaking supplies are sold. To begin, mix a 1:1 solution (for example, 400 grams of crystals in 400 milliliters of water). Next, dilute the solution to 2 percent (2 milliliters of solution per 100 milliliters of water).

All other things being equal, the same weight of wool (left) dyes to a deeper hue than silk (right).

Gradual color changes along the length of the fiber will create a gradient of colors in the spun yarn.

ACETIC ACID: Acetic acid can be obtained from photo- or chemical-supply houses. Dilute the acetic acid to 56 percent. Make up your fixative solution by using 2 milliliters of this acetic acid dilution per 100 milliliters of water.

VINEGAR: Household distilled white vinegar is a 5 percent solution of acetic acid. For 100 milliliters of water, you'll need about 1 milliliter of vinegar.

In preparation for dyeing, let the wetted fiber soak in the fixative solution for ten minutes so that it's thoroughly wet. If I'm using vinegar, which is volatile, I cover the bucket to help prevent evaporation. I use this soaking time to prepare the dyes.

Prepare the dye according to the manufacturer's instructions. For medium colors, I mix a 1 percent solution (1 gram of dye per 100 milliliters of liquid); for dark colors, a 2 percent solution (2 grams of dye per 100 milliliters of liquid).

Lay the yarn or fiber on a table covered with paper or plastic and apply the dyes with brushes. Be careful not to apply so much dye that pools form. Turn over the yarn or fiber and apply more dye if necessary for full penetration.

Wrap the yarn in plastic and steam on a rack placed over water heated to 212°F (100°C) for twenty minutes (longer at high altitudes). Allow it to cool to room temperature.

Rinse the yarn in warm to cool water until the rinse water runs clear.

Lay the fiber flat or hang skeins until thoroughly dry.

Fiber-Reactive Dyes

Silk can also be dyed with fiber-reactive dyes, which are typically used on cellulose-based fibers such as cotton, linen, and rayon. But these dyes work best in an alkaline (pH 8 or higher) solution, which is known to damage silk, especially when high temperatures are involved. It's important, therefore, to use a very weak (2 percent) alkaline solution, keep the temperature below 185°F (85°C), and to remove all alkaline compounds with thorough rinsing after the dye has set. Most fiber-reactive dyes fix within 24 to 48 hours.

I typically use fiber-reactive dyes for immersion dyeing of fiber, yarn, or fabric. There are two methods for applying fiber-reactive dyes: one requires heat; the other does not. For non-heated fixing (called "batching"), the dyes and fibers rest at room temperature 70°F (21°C) for 24 to 48 hours. Because there is no added heat, batched silk will sustain less damage from the alkaline used to fix fiber-reactive dyes. This is why I recommend using the nonheat (batching) process when using an alkaline fixative with fiber-reactive dyes. If you want to use heat, it's best to use an acid fixative.

Don't be afraid to try fiber-reactive dyes on silk. For years, I've had success using fiber-reactive dyes on commercial silk yarns. Just be sure to limit the amount of time the silk is in an alkaline solution and keep the temperature low.

Painting with Alkaline Fixative (Batching)

To begin, place the wet silk in a bucket and cover it with a 2 percent alkaline solution (2 grams of sodium carbonate to 100 milliliters of water).

Let the fiber soak for at least 10 minutes and up to an hour.

Prepare the dye according to the manufacturer's instructions. In general, I use a 1 percent solution for medium color depth and 2 percent for very dark colors. However, true black typically needs to be mixed at 3 percent or 4 percent; otherwise, it will turn out gray.

Cover the dyeing surface with plastic (I use kitchen plastic wrap on a table). Place the wet yarn on top of the wrap and apply the dye with thick brushes, using gentle stabbing motions as described on page 66.

Wrap the yarn in plastic and let it sit in a warm room for 24 to 48 hours, as recommended by the dye supplier.

Rinse the fiber until the water runs clear.

Lay the fiber flat or hang skeins until thoroughly dry.

Painting with an Acid Fixative

To begin, place the wet silk in a bucket and cover it with a 2 percent solution of citric or acetic acid.

Let the fiber soak for at least 10 minutes and up to an hour.

Prepare the dye according to the manufacturer's instructions. In general, I use a 1 percent solution for medium color depth and 2 percent for very dark colors. However, true black typically needs to be mixed at 3 percent or 4 percent; otherwise, it will turn out gray.

Cover the dyeing surface with plastic (I use kitchen plastic wrap on a table). Place the wet yarn on top of the wrap and apply the dye with thick brushes, using gentle stabbing motions as described on page 66.

Wrap the yarn in plastic, place the bundle on a steamer tray, and steam over boiling water for 20 minutes or the optimum time recommended by the supplier.

Immersion Dyeing with an Alkaline Fixative

Place the liquid, the premixed dye, and the yarn in a container large enough to hold the fiber comfortably when it's stirred.

Stir and rotate the yarn for 30 minutes while the dye "levels" or moves around to evenly cover the yarn.

Remove the yarn briefly and add a premixed 2 percent fixative (2 grams of sodium carbonate to 100 milliliters of water), the amount of which is determined by the weight of the fiber at a 1:1 ratio (100 grams of fiber to 100 milliliters of the 2 percent fixative solution).

Return the yarn and stir periodically to ensure even coverage until the desired depth of shade is achieved.

Rinse until the water runs clear.

Lay the fiber flat or hang skeins until thoroughly dry.

Immersion Dyeing with Acid Fixative

To begin, place the wet fiber in a nonreactive pot or container (such as stainless steel, glass, or enamel) of sufficient size to hold the silk plus enough liquid to prevent the fiber from touching the sides or bottom of the container (which could result in scorching). It's a good idea to place a steamer insert or rack in the bottom of the pot to ensure an inch (2.5 cm) or so of water between the silk and pot. For most of my immersion dyeing, I use a steamer unit that consists of an interior pan set in a water bath surrounded by a heating element. Because the interior pan is insulated by the water from the heating element, I don't have to worry as much about scorching.

For even dyeing, add about forty times as much water as there is fiber. For example, to dye 100 grams of silk evenly, you'll need 4,000 grams (4 liters) of water. If you want to end up with a semisolid color, use less water. However, be aware that if you use too little water, you may risk scorching the fiber.

Add a 2 percent acid fixative to help the dye attach to the fiber in a 1:1 ratio based on the weight of the fiber (100 grams of fiber to 100 milliliters of the 2 percent fixative solution).

Bring the temperature to simmer (about 200°F [93°C]) for at least twenty minutes or until the desired color is reached.

Let the yarn and solution cool to room temperature.

Lay the fiber flat or hang skeins until thoroughly dry.

Painting with Dye

In general each dye used for painting is weighed and mixed to the same depth of shade in a separate container. The yarn is soaked in a fixative solution of 2 percent citric acid, then stiff brushes are used to apply the dye and help it penetrate to the undersurface of the yarn.

Commercially available dyes are weighed to mix to the same depth of shade in each container. Yarns to be painted are soaked in a fixative solution of 2 percent citric acid. Stiff brushes help the dye penetrate to the undersurface of the yarn.

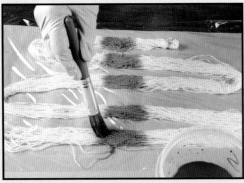

Use a stiff brush to stamp each color as desired onto the wet fiber.

The colors will blend together where they intersect.

Paint all the colors on one side of the warp chain or skein.

Carefully turn over the warp chain or skein and re-apply dye to areas where penetration is lacking.

Wrap the dyed yarn in plastic to prevent the colors from running while the yarn is heated and the dye sets.

A Fiber-Reactive Dyeing Cautionary Tale

I wove the scarf shown below in a black-and-white doubleweave pattern on eight shafts, with the intent of painting the white areas to create a more complex pattern. I dyed the black yarn in a 4 percent immersion dyebath (4 grams of dye powder to every 100 milliliters of liquid, which, in this case, was water). I heated the bath, then added a mild acid and heated it for about 30 minutes.

After weaving the fabric, I painted a few samples using acid dyes, a mild acidic fixative (mild acid), and a thickener of sodium alginate to prevent the dye from spreading or bleeding. I soon realized that it would be easier to first overdye the scarf pale yellow, then just paint on the other colors.

I had a fiber-reactive yellow dye already mixed, so I decided to use it in an immersion bath with a sodium carbonate (alkaline) fixative and placed the pot on heat to speed up the process. To my dismay, the scarf came out of the dyebath obviously damaged. The surface appeared "stone washed," with a faded, rough and worn look.

I painted on the rest of the design, and learned a valuable lesson: Do not add heat when using an alkaline substance on silk.

The black yarn and the black-and-white samples in the upper right show the undamaged silk after it had been heated while dyed with acid dyes. The multicolored scarf in the foreground has a faded, rough, and worn look caused by overdyeing the silk by heating it in an alkaline solution.

Natural Dyes

Natural dye substances have been used for both immersion dyeing and painting on silk for centuries. However, most of the fixatives (called mordants) used with natural dyes are alkaline, so the temperatures at which the dyes are fixed should be kept as low as possible.

Sodium hydrosulfite, lye, or ammonia are typically used as reducing agents for indigo dyeing. All of these are alkaline substances that are corrosive to silk. Take care to use them in sufficient, but not excessive, amounts and to use a low temperature range. Consult natural-dye books (see Resources) for information.

Potassium aluminum (alum) is another alkaline substance that should be used sparingly with silk. Alum mordant can be used for many natural-dye substances, such as madder, onion skins, and coreopsis flowers. It's usually used in a pre-mordant bath before immersion into a dyebath or before painting the fiber or yarn.

Solar Dyeing

Any dyestuff can be fixed by solar heat. Simply prepare the silk with the appropriate fixative, paint or soak the fiber with the dye solution, and place the fiber or yarn in a glass container that, in turn, is placed in a covered black container (or black plastic bag) in bright sun for as long as necessary to obtain the desired depth of color.

If you use an alkaline fixative (for fiber-reactive or natural dyes), keep the dye temperature at or below 120°F (49°C), and check at intervals until the desired depth of shade is reached. For fiber-reactive dyes, this will take at least 24 to 48 hours. For many natural dye substances, it could be several weeks. Don't let the dye liquid become cloudy and watch for any signs of degradation, molds, or scum forming on the surface. If this occurs, wash the yarn immediately.

Many natural substances such as lichens (green), madder root (rust), and indigo (blue) require an alkaline fixative, which can be harmful to silk fibers when heated.

CHAPTER FOUR

Using Handspun Silk Yarn

4

"*Silk is naturally lustrous*, but must be woven in such a manner as to allow as large as possible a number of threads close together to form a smooth surface before the light can be adequately reflected in it."

—*Ciba Review #11, page 373*

I'm a big advocate of using handspun yarn. As spinners, the best way to determine the success of a yarn is by its utility. Make things and use them to see how your yarn behaves, in use and over time. As I've used my textiles, I've made changes to the way I spin and how I use that yarn to make fabric. Only through using the yarn will you be able to determine if it suits your purposes.

In addition to visual examination, trust your fingers and hands to tell you what's right or wrong about your fabric. Then make the necessary adjustments to your spinning, weaving, knitting, etc.—and make something else. Ultimately, you'll spin just the right yarn for whatever it is you want to make.

Weaving

SILK HAS BEEN USED AS A WEAVING yarn for centuries. Until just a few hundred years ago, however, most weaving was done with reeled silk yarn. The leftover waste was used primarily as batting or stuffing; only a very small amount was spun. But carding and spinning equipment developed during the Industrial Revolution made it much easier to process silk waste into yarn. Initially, spun silk was used just as weft in fabrics of lesser quality. However, as spinning equipment improved, so did the yarn; eventually, spun silk gained acceptance as both warp and weft.

Maintaining Luster

Spun silk is inherently less lustrous than reeled silk. The shorter filaments used for spun silk interrupt the surface of the yarn and break up the reflection of light. Silk is also more likely to pill in spun form: the tiny fibers work their way out of the twist, become abraded, and roll into pills on the surface of the fabric. Therefore, spun silk is often relegated to weave structures in which luster isn't as important, such as velvet, and as the weft in lesser quality silk yardage.

As handspinners and handweavers, however, we can help preserve the luster that's the hallmark of silk. We can enhance the luster by putting tighter twist in the yarn. The finest silk fabrics with the most drape also need plenty of twist. Spun silk is most often plied so that the fiber is more closely aligned with the length of the yarn (see page 52)—the fibers that are most parallel to the length of yarn catch and reflect the most light.

Silk also appears shiniest when closely packed in the warp or weft, as well as in weave structures that have the fewest breaks, or intersections, to interrupt the reflection of light. Therefore, warp- or weft-faced fabrics, in which only the warp or weft yarn is visible, have more sheen than balanced plain weave, in which the warp and weft appear in equal amounts. Moreover, a plain-weave structure deflects the light, which reduces luster, as demonstrated in the sample at upper right. The luster of silk is also more apparent in satin weave, warp or weft brocade, and some twill structures.

The addition of color can further accentuate or diminish the luster of silk. In the sample at center right, the close sett and twill structure in the dyed yarns reflect more light, and they appear visually prominent against the darker background. The darker areas, woven in plain weave, have less luster and recede visually, further accentuating the bright-colored stripes. Two-ply bombyx was used for the warp and weft in this sample.

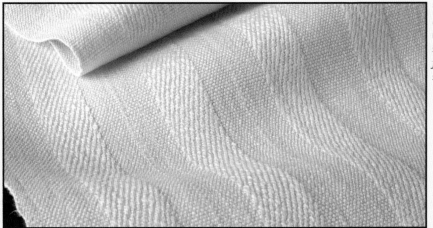

Closely sett twill stripes appear more lustrous than the plain-weave areas in this fabric. The same two-ply bombyx was used for the warp and weft in this sample.

The twill structure in the brightly colored yarns in this sample reflect more light and appear more lustrous against the dark background.

The combination of sett and weave structure reduced the luster in my first silk scarf.

Experiments and Examples

In addition to weaving samples, I often weave scarves or shawls. They don't have to be a particular width or length, and they're relatively quick to spin yarn for, set up on the loom, and weave. The ends can be hemmed or twisted into fringe. Scarves and shawls are always useful, and each one offers a lesson in fabric appearance, hand, and behavior. In addition, they provide nice opportunities to experiment with weave structure, sett, weft size, and color.

The first silk scarf that I spun and wove was a disappointment. It exemplifies several ways that I managed to obscure the luster so prized in silk fibers. First, I spun tussah fiber, which isn't as smooth or fine as bombyx and which reflects less light. Second, I didn't add enough twist as I spun, and the fine filament ends escaped to create a halo of fine fibers on the surface (called fibrillation). Third, I chose a broken twill weave structure that separated the yarns into small units that refracted the light and created more sparkle than sheen on the surface of the fabric.

Unhappy with my initial results, I set about spinning and weaving a number of samples to compare factors that affect luster. To begin, I spun the same tussah fiber into a tightly twisted and plied yarn, used a close sett of 40 ends per inch, and wove it in plain weave. The enhanced sheen in this fabric is much closer to my original intent, although both

fabrics were woven from yarn spun from tussah bricks; two-ply for the warp and singles for the weft. This proved that tight twist and close sett are key to good luster.

Next, I tried combining commercial black silk yarn with a more textured yarn that I spun from hankies. I wove the black yarn in plain weave and the textured hankie yarn in twill. Even though the hankie yarn is textured and bumpy, the closely sett twill structure causes the yarns to lie on the surface of the fabric and enhances what shine there is.

By this point, I knew that close-sett warp-dominant weave structures would push the shiny yarns right next to each other and create a surface that would reflect light and reveal the luster. I wondered what would happen if the close-sett twill yarn were smooth, tightly spun bombyx instead of the more textured yarn I had spun from hankies. I spun and wove samples of white bombyx in plain weave and twill. As expected, the visible warp and weft intersections in the plain-weave area caused the light to disperse. The plain-weave fabric isn't as lustrous as the closer-sett twill fabric.

To see how color might affect things, I combined black silk in plain weave with bright colors in twill. Visually, the black appears to recede while the colors pop forward. Again, there's plenty of luster in the closer-packed twill areas; the black yarn obscures any luster in the plain-weave areas.

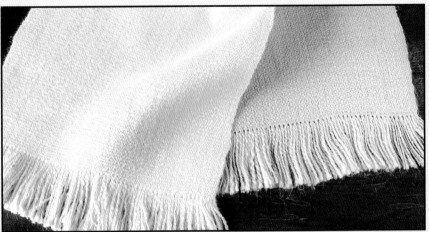

Plain weave, in a very close sett of 40 ends per inch, enhances the luster in the sample on the left as compared to the broken twill fabric on the right.

A close sett and a twill structure enhance the luster in the red silk spun from hankies.

The luster is more apparent in the twill stripes than the plain-weave areas in this bombyx scarf.

However, if a close sett is used, even plain-weave fabrics can exhibit good luster. When the warp yarns are spaced very close together, the effect is similar to satin and twill structures.

Keep in mind that the quality of the silk fiber will also affect its luster. For uniform luster, use silk fiber from a single source. I spun all of the purple yarn in the scarf at the bottom of page 77 with the same amount of twist and ply, and I used the same sett for all of the stripes. But, I used a lower-quality (grade C) silk brick for the yarn in the painted-warp sections. There is less luster and shine in these sections and the yarn shrank more, producing a slight seersucker effect in the finished scarf.

Learning how close to thread, or sett, silk on the loom requires abandoning some of the rules established for other fibers. Silk isn't wool, nor is it cashmere, alpaca, or even cotton, though it most closely resembles cotton. Woven silk fabric should feel a bit stiff when it first comes off the loom, even after washing and pressing. If the fabric is too soft and drapey right off the loom, it will relax into a sleazy and limp cloth with use and wear.

The warp for all three of the fabrics shown on page 79 were spun with the same 80/20 merino-silk blend, but in different colorways. The yarn measured 18 wraps per inch. All three were woven with the same 48/2 merino weft. The only difference was in how closely the warp was sett. All three fabrics are perfectly usable, but looser setts result in looser, less durable fabrics, which will affect the end use. Sometimes, the only way to know the best sett for your project is to sample.

Warp Sizing

If you plan to use silk singles in a warp, you may want to apply a sizing before dressing the loom. Gelatin makes a simple sizing agent. Mix it with at least double the water called for when used as a thickener for food. Soak the skeins or run the threads through this solution as a warp chain. Hang to dry, allowing the excess sizing to drip off, while separating the yarn as it dries to prevent it from sticking to itself. Sized threads will be stiff, but the sizing will wash out during finishing.

The processing of cocoons can leave a small amount of sericin coating on some of the fibers, which is more prevalent in some preparations. If you plan to weave with undyed silk yarn, there may be no need for additional degumming. The sericin will act as sizing in warp yarns and make them easier to work with. It can be removed later in a degumming bath.

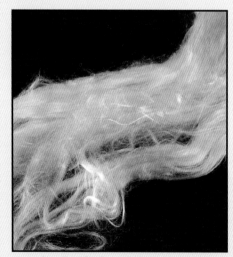

Some fiber benefits from degumming before spinning. Otherwise, clumps and areas that are stuck together can be hard to draft.

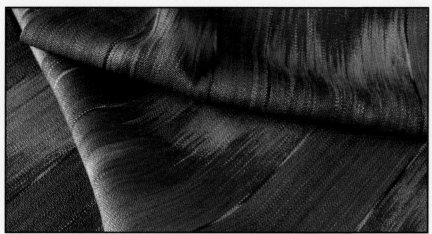

Luster is evident in this close-sett plain-weave fabric. The warp is fine two-ply bombyx (40 wpi) sett at 48 epi. The weft is a fine 20/2 cotton.

The fiber spun for the purple stripe (left) was of better quality than that spun for the orange and gold stripe (right). The better-grade silk appears more lustrous and shrank less.

Remember the denim jeans of the 1970s that we bought stiff and broke in with wear and washing? Today's jeans are made from thinner cloth or cloth that's been "stone washed" into softness. They don't wear as well, have less body, and are less durable than their predecessors.

Silk fabric is much the same. After years of wearing my silk scarves, they've become extraordinarily soft and have incredible drape. But they show no signs of wear. After more than a decade of wear, they look as good as the day they were new, but they feel better every day.

On to Garments

After weaving four large scarves from my handspun silk, I decided it was time to make a full garment. I've made a variation of a hanten kimono, or working jacket (see page 106), from a variety of my handspun fibers. This simple garment, consisting of relatively few narrow strips of fabric, would be excellent for my first silk garment. It's loosely fitted, requires few cuts or curved pieces, and involves little waste of precious handspun, handwoven yardage.

Based on my experience with silk scarves, I knew I wanted to use silk spun from a single source, spin that fiber into a fine yarn with ample twist, add lots of twist in the plying, and choose a weft that would help the fabric drape. In this case, I chose to spin bombyx from silk bricks for the warp. For weft, I used a commercial three-ply silk in about the same size as 60/2 commercial silk yarn. I knew that the weft would have to be finer if it wasn't to inhibit the drape.

I set the warp closely for a warp-dominant plain weave that I knew would provide excellent warpwise drape, as well as an interesting visual component to the garment construction. It took me about six months to spin the silk for the jacket. I dyed the yarn, wove the fabric, and sewed the jacket without serious difficulty. Although it felt nice to wear and had a good hand, it was visually disappointing. The lively color had an exuberance that, though acceptable in a small accessory such as a scarf, seemed too busy as an overall pattern on a garment.

No matter, I'd make another. For warp in the second kimono, I used combed top that was a blend of silk and cashmere that I'd obtained at a weaver's yard sale. I dyed this yarn in more subdued colors. For the weft, I used the same three-ply bombyx that I used in the first kimono. This jacket was much more successful. The cashmere added soft fibrillation to the surface of the fabric and the dyeing was better suited to a garment.

These three fabrics were woven with the same warp and weft yarns (but different colors) and woven at different setts. Left to right: 15 ends per inch, 20 ends per inch, 24 ends per inch (fabric woven by Eileen Lee).

After more than fifteen years of use, the drape in these silk scarves only improves. Thanks to the close sett, they've held up well and show no signs of wear.

Tussah retains its luster and drape after twelve years of use and wear.

I was anxious to make another. For the warp in the third kimono, I spun bombyx silk at 40 wpi and sett it at 48 epi. For the weft, I used commercial 140/2 bombyx, which turned out to be a mistake. The weft was so fine that the finished fabric was too lightweight—it was better suited for lingerie fabric. The weaving was a frustrating and tedious process. The fine weft broke as I wove, and I had to weave slowly and carefully, making sure each shed was fully cleared before sending the shuttle across.

Over the years, I've made several other kimonos, always keeping in mind the two lessons I'd learned: the color needs to feel cohesive for the large scale of a garment, and the weft needs to be thick enough to impart suitable weight to the fabric.

My first kimono fabric has a nice hand and drapes well, but the bold narrow stripes make it visually too "busy."

The more analogous colors in my second kimono fabric suited both the garment and the fiber.

My third kimono fabric has the same grist yarns as the first kimono, but a finer weft made a fabric that was too lightweight for a jacket.

I've found several wefts suitable for a wearable, durable jacket fabric: 10/1 noil silk, 20/1 noil silk, and 20/2 cotton. Because weft size helps determine the hand of the fabric, I usually choose a finer weft to give drape in the body of a jacket and a heavier weft to make sturdier fabric for the bands. The bands take more wear and need to be more stable. They hold the shape of the garment and provide a secure base for closures, such as buttons and loops. I've come to prefer a "toothy" weft (one with surface texture) that holds better at seams than the slick bombyx I used in the first two jackets. For a garment in which the seams will undergo stress, I prefer cotton, silk noil, or wool wefts.

Fine bombyx silk is a suitable weft for scarves or shawls that don't have seams.

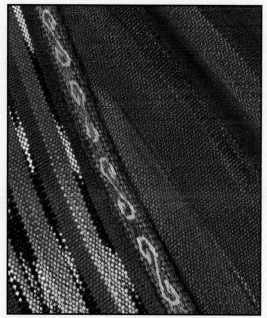

I used a heavier cotton weft for the front band of this jacket, which gets more wear and provides stability at the front edge.

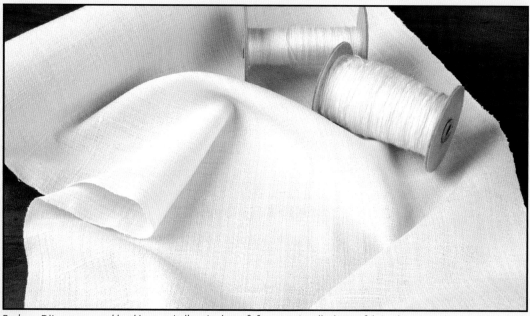

Barbara DiJeannene used hankies to spindle-spin the weft for exceptionally drapey fabric; the warp is her two-ply handspun bombyx silk.

Three-ply or tightly twisted two-ply yarns hold up to weaving sturdy fabrics and abrasive techniques.

Although I generally weave with two-ply silk, there are some cases when three-ply is suitable and, perhaps, preferable. I use three-ply tussah for the warp in pile weaves. It's sturdy and withstands the abrasion, tension, and heavy beating required for this type of weaving. But it's still supple enough to allow for a fluid finished fabric. I also use three-ply yarn for tablet weaving for the same reason—a close sett and the friction of the turning tablets can abrade the warp yarn.

In tablet weaving, a close sett and the friction of the turning tablets can abrade the warp yarn.

Pile fabrics require sturdy warps, such as the three-ply used here, that can withstand abrasive beating under tight tension.

Finishing Woven Fabric

To finish woven fabric, I fill my washing machine with hot water and ½ cup (120 milliliters) vinegar, add the fabric, and let it soak for at least 20 minutes to ensure that the fiber is saturated to the core. Then I turn on the agitator (my top-loader has a column agitator) for 5 minutes. If I think that the fabric has fulled enough, I spin out the excess water in the machine. If I think it hasn't fulled enough, I set the timer and check every 5 minutes until I'm satisfied with the results. I examine the surface of the fabric as it's finishing to make sure there isn't too much surface fibrillation and to make sure that the reed marks are gone. Silk doesn't felt, but the warp and weft will bloom and shift in the washing process, making a smoother, more cohesive fabric.

I put the spun-dry fabric in the dryer for 5 minutes on high heat, then press it with a medium iron to dry the surface and bring out the shine. The vinegar from the finishing bath helps neutralize any alkaline residue from the previous water bath and helps prevent damage to the fibers as it is ironed.

Finally, I hang the fabric over a thick rod (I suspend a 2-inch [5-centimeter] diameter PVC pipe from the ceiling in my studio) to fully dry, which can take a few days. This way, there's no chance of the fabric developing wrinkles.

Keep in mind that yarns of differing fiber content may behave differently in the finishing. Watch for differential shrinkage, even after the yarns have been washed and pre-shrunk before you wind the warp. To mitigate differential shrinkage potential, spread different yarns across the warp in narrow units.

One of the silk-cashmere yarns in this yak-silk and silk-cashmere fabric didn't shrink as much as the others during fabric finishing, which caused a slight puckering in the wide light tan stripes.

Silk Blends in Weaving

Silk is commonly blended with wool, cashmere, yak, or bison. These fine animal fibers have crimp and elasticity, are warm for their weight, and usually impart a fuzzy surface to the yarn and fabrics made from them. Silk will mitigate these factors, adding weight, drape, luster, and a smoother surface.

I spin blended fibers as if they were pure silk—a fine yarn with plenty of twist. No matter what it's blended with, silk is a very fine fiber that will fibrillate, or pill, in yarns with less twist. It's important to note that the soft hand produced by fine fibers is the result of the inherent properties of those fibers, not the amount of twist. Tighter twist doesn't result in stiff fabrics if you begin with soft fiber; soft fiber results in soft fabric after proper finishing.

However, I was curious to see if there would be differential shrinkage between the fibers in a blend and, if so, how that would affect the finished fabric. To find out, I spun a series of blended yarns and wove samples from them.

Wool-Silk Blends

For the first sample, I combined a commercial blend of 85 percent Bluefaced Leicester with 15 percent silk in a two-ply yarn at 17 wraps per inch (wpi). I threaded the blend for plain weave at a sett of 15 epi and used a fine 48/2 commercial wool for weft. The resulting fabric has a textured pebbly surface. I wondered if this texture was because of differential shrinkage in the wool-silk blend.

To test whether the textured surface resulted from differential shrinkage in the wool-silk blend yarn, I wove another fabric using a blend of 80 percent merino and 20 percent silk yarn of the same grist and at the same sett as before. I used the same yarn in the weft. I also wove the beginning of the sample with a cotton weft of the same grist. The portion of the sample with the merino-silk weft has a pebbly surface while the portion with the cotton weft fabric did not pebble.

Alpaca and silk complement each other nicely. Both have luster, drape well, and work well in woven structures. The interaction of warp and weft can help prevent the fiber from elongating during use. Spun by Eileen Lee.

I combined several dyed colors of Bluefaced Leicester silk with warp-painted yarn for this jacket fabric. The yarn wrapped at 17 wpi, was sett at 15 wpi, and woven with a 48/2 merino weft.

I began to wonder if it was the weft, rather than the blended fibers, that was shrinking, and, if so, would it make a difference if I used a closer sett so that there would be less space for the weft to shift and potentially shrink. For the next sample, I used the same 80/20 merino-silk blend in the warp and the same weft, but this time at a sett of 20 epi, which is what I'd use for a pure silk fabric with a yarn of same grist (18 wpi). There's no sign of differential shrinkage, which I now think was due to the weft in the pebbly fabrics. I've concluded that if fabrics woven of blends are treated like pure silk, they will behave like silk, but will produce a warmer, fuzzy surface.

Cotton-Silk Blends

Silk and cotton fibers are very much alike. Both are fine and slick and neither has crimp nor scales. The fiber in silk top generally has a longer staple length than cotton. But silk is cut to length for spinning, and the shorter lengths are ideal for blending with cotton. Fabrics woven from cotton–silk blends are soft and supple, but they have a bit less luster than a fabric woven of silk alone.

Both cotton and silk can be cool to wear in summer and warm in winter. Silk makes the shorter cotton fibers easier to spin, while cotton is less slick, which makes it easier to draft fine silk fibers.

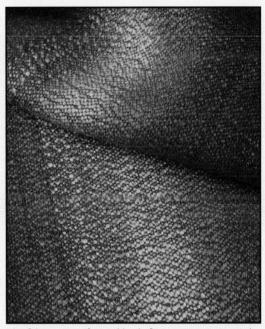

This fabric, woven from a blend of 80 percent merino and 20 percent silk in both warp and weft, developed a pebbly surface during finishing.

At a closer sett, the warp yarns didn't have as much room to shrink and distort, and the fabric has a smoother surface.

Knitting

'MOST OF TODAY'S KNITTING YARNS are generally softly spun, lofty, and elastic. Because the fine fibers fibrillate, silk doesn't handle well when spun into this type of soft yarn, especially at thicker grists. The fibers tend to work their way out of the yarn and form pills on the surface.

Instead, silk needs substantial twist, either in the initial spin or in the ply (or both) to hold it in the yarn. I prefer to spin silk in fine, tightly twisted singles and then ply two or more singles together to achieve the desired grist. An advantage to tightly twisted yarn is that there is better stitch definition.

Because silk has less elasticity than wool, the structure of the knitting must provide the necessary elasticity. Ribbing, cables, and stretchy stitches are best for this purpose. Because silk has incredible drape, it's ideal for knitted garments such as scarves, shawls, and tunics that don't need to maintain a particular shape.

Maintaining Luster

The same silk yarn will not appear as lustrous in knitted fabrics as it does in close-sett woven ones. This is because knitted stitches (even tightly knitted ones) do not have the long parallel arrangement that deflects light so beautifully in woven fabrics. Therefore, although knitted silk fabrics may have some luster and shine, their primary appeal is in the drape and feel of the fabric, which is wonderful.

Knitted and woven samples of the same tussah silk yarns illustrate how the technique itself influences the appearance and hand of the final product.

Experiments and Examples

I wanted to knit with handspun silk of various grists to compare how the different grists would behave in knitted fabric. For each sample, I spun my usual singles, then plied as I would for weaving.

For the first sample, I spun two-ply bombyx at 7,500 yards (6,858 meters) per pound. I used size U.S. 8/0 (.5 mm) needles to knit a stockinette-stitch swatch that was twenty-five stitches wide and thirty rows tall. The swatch measured 1⅜ inches (3.5 centimeters) wide and 1¼ inches (3.2 centimeters) tall before washing and 1¼ inches (3.2 centimeters) wide. It measured 1⅛ inches (2.8 centimeters) tall after washing, with a post-washing gauge of twenty stitches per inch (2.5 centimeters).

For the second sample, I spun tussah at 4,500 yards (4, 115 meters) per pound. I used size U.S. 5/0 (1 mm) needles to knit a stockinette-stitch swatch that was twenty-five stitches wide and forty rows tall. The swatch measured 1⅞ inches (4.7 centimeters) square before washing and 1¾ inches (4.4 centimeters) wide. It measured 1⅝ inches (4.1 centimeters) tall after washing, with a post-washing gauge of fourteen and a quarter stitches per inch (2.5 centimeters).

I didn't enjoy knitting either of these samples. I had trouble seeing the stitches clearly, and my needles split the yarn often enough to annoy me. Clearly, the yarn needed more twist in both the singles and plying. To top it off, the fine yarn and tiny needles caused cramps in my hands. After knitting these two swatches, I knew I would never try to replicate the fine-gauge stockings or mittens in vintage patterns.

I turned instead to sampling for a lace scarf or shawl that could be knitted on larger needles, such as size U.S. 00 or 0 (1.75 or 2 mm). For the next sample, I spun tussah into tighter

These swatches illustrate how the types of silk and number of plies handle during knitting and finishing. From left to right on this page: two-ply bombyx, two-ply tussah, three-ply tussah. From left to right on opposite page: the same three-ply tussah, four-ply tussah, and four-ply cabled tussah yarn. In general, I prefer multiple-ply yarns for knitting.

singles that I twisted tightly into a three-ply yarn at 3,000 yards (2,743 meters) per pound. I used size U.S. 00 (1.75 mm) needles to knit a swatch that was twenty-five stitches wide and thirty-five rows tall. The swatch measured 2⅜ inches (6 centimeters) wide and 2 inches (5 centimeters) tall before washing and 2⅛ inches (5.4 centimeters) wide and 1⅞ inches (4.7 centimeters) tall after washing, with a post-washing gauge of eleven and three-quarters stitches per inch (2.5 centimeters).

Next, I made a tightly spun four-ply yarn from the tussah that measured 2,250 yards (2,057 meters) per pound. I used size U.S. 00 (1.75 mm) needles to knit a swatch that was twenty-five stitches wide and thirty-three rows tall. The swatch measured 2⅝ inches (6.7 centimeters) wide and 2⅜ inches (6.0 centimeters) tall before washing and 2⁷⁄₁₆ inches (6.2 centimeters) wide and 2⅛ inches (5.4 centimeters) tall after washing, with a

post-washing gauge of ten stitches per inch (2.5 centimeters).

Both of these yarns have promise. The stitches were much easier to see, the yarn didn't split, and the fabric felt good, draped well, and was pliable and comfortable. Another advantage to using multiple plies is that you can introduce subtle color variations by changing the color of one strand at a time (see the rainbow shawl on page 118 and the knitted blue and orange bag on page 113).

For the final swatch, I spun a tussah four-ply cabled yarn at 2,500 yards (2,286 meters) per pound. I used size U.S. 0000 (1.25 mm) needles to knit a swatch that was twenty-five stitches wide and thirty-five rows tall. The swatch measured 2¼ inches (5.5 centimeters) square before washing and 2 inches (5 centimeters) wide and 2⅛ inches (5.4 centimeters) tall after washing, with a post-washing gauge of eleven stitches per inch (2.5 centimeters).

Cabled yarns of any fiber can be very firm and sturdy, and they're ideal for showing off stitch patterns. This silk sample is no different. I used a four-ply cabled yarn to crochet the evening bag shown at right and on page 117 (see page 93 for details about crochet yarns).

Next, I explored commercial knitting yarns. These yarns run the gamut from softly spun singles to multiple-ply yarns in various configurations of twist and ply—soft and tight twist; single and multiple plies. I bought several that looked promising and knitted samples with them. Commercial yarns are a good place to get inspiration and ideas, whether for weaving, knitting, or embroidery.

After all these samples, I came to the conclusion that my preference is to spin the singles fine and with plenty of twist and then to create the final yarn with plying variations, depending on the desired end use.

The firm fabric in this bag was knitted with a yarn made up of four plies of fine singles. The fabric holds its shape but has the drape and shine we expect from silk.

I took inspiration from a commercial yarn when sampling yarn construction for knitting. Top: Louisa Harding seven-ply Mulberry. Bottom from left to right: six singles plied together, seven two-ply strands plied together, seven two-ply strands simply held together.

Examine a commercial silk yarn that you like for inspiration. The commercial yarn shown at the top of the photo at the bottom of page 90 (Louisa Harding seven-ply Mulberry) is composed of twelve two-ply strands plied together with seven strands in one bundle and five strands in the other. I spun a simple six-ply (six singles plied together) sample and two samples of seven two-ply strands: one in which the seven strands are plied together and one in which the seven strands were simply held together. In all cases, the multiple strands resulted in a yarn with suitable grist that would provide both body and resilience in a knitted garment.

In general, I found commercial singles yarn too soft and slippery. These yarns tended to result in fabrics that pilled even as they were knitted. The multiple-strand yarns, however, had me spinning and plying lots of options.

To manage the multiple strands of silk singles necessary to make a plied yarn, I first wind the singles into individual balls. I place the balls into a basket and wind them together into a single ball. Finally, I add twist to all of the strands at once. Imagine the color possibilities when so many strands are involved!

Finishing Knitted Fabric

To finish knitted silk fabric, I fill my laundry sink with hot soapy water, add the knitted piece, and let it soak for at least twenty minutes. Then I remove the garment, drain the water, refill the sink with fresh hot water, and add the garment for a good rinsing. I squeeze out excess water and hang or lay it flat to dry. If I'm dealing with 100 percent silk, I may press the fabric with a hot iron before hanging it over a rod to fully dry.

I don't worry about preventing water—hot or cold—from running directly on 100 percent silk yarn, woven fabric, or knitted garment. Silk doesn't felt. However, if the yarn is a blend that contains fibers that might felt, I take care to remove the fabric before running water, maintain a consistent water temperature, and avoid rubbing or agitating the fabric.

Ripping Out Knitted Silk

Knitted silk stitches are very slippery. If you have to rip out to fix an error, use a hot iron and damp pressing cloth on the part of the fabric that will *not* be ripped out. This will block those stitches and help keep them stationary long enough for you to return them to the needle after you've ripped down to the mistake.

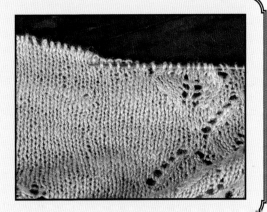

Silk Blends in Knitting

For knitting yarns, silk is blended with many animal fibers—merino, cashmere, Bluefaced Leicester, and camel, to name a few. These fibers add warmth and a halo of soft fibers to the silk. For its part, the silk adds luster, strength, drape, and durability to the other fibers. Some blends are more homogenous than others, but each can make lovely knitwear.

Keep in mind that silk fiber is heavier and lacks the elasticity of wool. It therefore won't recover its shape once stretched. To compensate, you might want to knit silk at a tighter gauge (more stitches per inch) than you would for a wool yarn of the same grist. I find that silk-blend yarns are best for knitted items that don't need to be a particular size, such as scarves, shawls, and baby blankets.

The weight of silk in a blended yarn will change how the knitted fabric behaves. It behaves best in stitch patterns that help stabilize the knitted fabric.

I swatched a variety of commercial silk-blend knitting yarns to see which types of blends I would prefer. Regardless of the type of blend, I discovered that I prefer those composed of fine singles and multiple plies to thicker yarns composed of fewer plies. Softly spun or larger grist yarns lacked body and had a much greater tendency to pill. For example, 100 percent Bluefaced Leicester spins into a nice sport-weight yarn, but if 15 percent silk is added, I think it behaves better in a laceweight yarn.

I now spin silk blends as if they were pure silk. I spin fine singles that have a bit more twist than I would use for the "blended-in" fiber alone. In short, I spin to the silk component in the blend. I impart substantial twist in the singles and ply the singles firmly together for tight, well-twisted yarn. I recommend plying two strands together for laceweight yarns and adding plies as needed to create fatter yarns.

Silk adds drape and sheen, both of which are attractive in knitted shawls and scarves.

Dee Jones used a stablilizing stitch pattern to maintain body in this silk-blend scarf.

Other Applications

Crochet

Commercial crochet yarns are tightly spun and plied for maximum abrasion resistance (these yarns also exhibit excellent stitch definition). In the process of forming crochet stitches, loops are formed through which the hook passes at least two, and sometimes many, times. Each pass of the hook rubs and can abrade the yarn. Because silk is best spun and plied firmly, it's ideal for crocheted shawls, edgings, and doilies. Upon immediate finishing, the piece might feel a bit stiff, but with a little use and wear, the drape and hand we expect from silk will become apparent.

Commercial crochet cottons are typically spun in the S (counterclockwise) direction and plied in the Z (clockwise) direction. The process of creating crocheted stitches twists the yarns and, depending on the twist direction in the yarn and the worker's motions, twist can be added or subtracted from the yarn as the stitches are formed.

I typically spin in the Z direction and ply in the S direction, which is counter to commercial crochet yarns. However, if I make a cable yarn by plying two 2-ply yarns together, the final twist is in the Z direction and the results are the same.

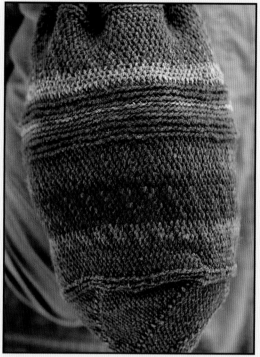

Cabled yarns make very sturdy crochet fabrics.

Generally speaking, any technique can be worked with yarn spun in either direction, but the direction may affect the outcome. The manner in which you hold the working yarn and the direction in which you grab the yarn for each stitch may slightly untwist or add twist to the yarn as you work. And this can affect how the finished project behaves and how it looks.

Embroidery and Needlepoint

Silk, both reeled and spun, has long been used in many cultures as embellishment for clothing, religious textiles, and ceremonial garments. Yarns laid close together on the surface of the fabric show the luster and sheen of silk to best advantage. However, these yarns are subject to considerable abrasion in the mere act of drawing them in and out of the background fabric. Therefore, silk yarns commercially produced for these techniques are typically the stronger reeled, not spun, variety.

To approximate the smooth surface of reeled yarns, spinners might wish to be aware of the "nap" of the fibers. The direction in which the fibers lie should be controlled, in both the spinning and plying, and noted so that it can be used to its best advantage in needlework.

Yarn spun for needlework does benefit by being repackaged before plying: spin the yarn, wind off onto storage bobbins for plying, and mark the skeins for eventual needlework to indicate the nap, or direction of twist.

Reeled silk yarns used in embroidery have very little inserted twist, which allows the filaments to lie close together in all their lustrous glory. Doubled (plied) yarns are typically used in areas where texture and sparkle are desired. These are the yarns that spinners can emulate.

Tightly spun silk singles can create very smooth embroidered surfaces if they're placed close to one another as for satin stitch, as used by Deb Menz in her Carbonated Colors on page 128. If plied silk had been used, the reflected light would be interrupted, resulting in less shine and luster.

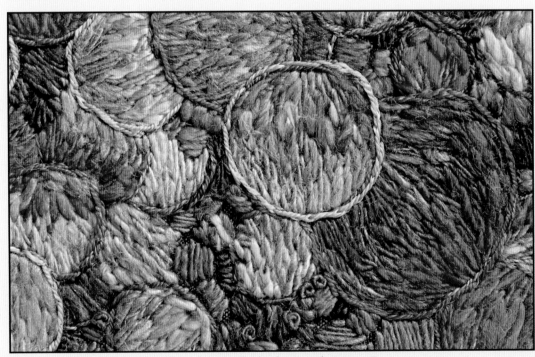

Detail of embroidery stitches in Deb Menz's Carbonated Colors (see also page 128).

Kumihimo and Other Braiding Techniques

Kumihimo is a Japanese braiding technique worked on a braiding stand or a portable cardboard or foam disc. Groups of reeled silk strands, called bundles, that have very little twist are traditionally used for this technique. The smooth strands lie parallel to one another and reflect as much light as possible. You can use spun-silk bundles instead of reeled silk, but the light will not reflect as much. Using multiple strands for color and bundle size makes the braids almost infinitely variable.

Plied silk or stranded bundles of several strands—either singles or plied, but not twisted together—work well for other braiding techniques, such as finger-loop braiding. However, silk singles should be tightly twisted to ensure the fibrillates are captured so that braiding is easier and will hold up through the twisting and untwisting caused by braid formation.

In kumihimo, multiple strands blend colors and bring the yarn to a suitable grist for braiding.

Finger-loop braids can be made with thrums for small projects such as this wrist distaff.

Inkle Bands

Silk ribbons and bands can be made with any number of plies: I commonly use two-ply and three-ply yarns. For most simple bands, two-ply yarn is sufficient. For bands with pick-up patterning, I use double strands or multiple plies so that they're at least double the size of the background thread.

It's possible to weave inkle bands with singles as long as the singles are well twisted. The abrasion that occurs during the exchange of the working yarns at each shed change means that smoother, tighter twist will hold up better under the process and hinder the weaving less. You might wish to size a singles warp if you plan to use it in a close-sett band. Well-spun and tightly plied yarns need no sizing.

Inkle bands use two- and three-ply yarns in different applications—for pick-up and background yarns, as well as plain-woven bands.

The heavier grist of the three-ply pattern yarns stands out nicely against the two-ply background in this inkle band.

96

Tablet Weaving

Strong two- and three-ply yarns are best for tablet weaving. Moreover, if there isn't sufficient twist, the yarns can become abraded during use and untwist during the twining process and not survive the making. As the tablets are turned forward and then back, twist is added and subtracted from the warp yarn. Plied yarns hold up better to the friction of the cards against the warp yarns, the changes in twist caused by the rotating tablets, and the tension of the twisted strands as the weaving progresses. Singles are not a good choice, no matter how much twist was originally inserted, because they can come unspun during the weaving process.

Tablet weaving has long been used for bindings and animal trappings. Because it produces multiple layers, it's strong and durable. If one thread of a four-thread bundle breaks during use, the remaining three will hold it together. Even if two threads are abraded from the edge of a band, the remaining two will keep the band intact. Therefore, tablet weaving is useful for bag handles, badge holders, and any other sturdy band that needs to withstand abrasion and stress.

These tablet bands are woven with sturdy yarns. From left to right: relatively thick two-ply, thinner two-ply, and three-ply yarns.

Two-ply silk was used for the tablet-woven handle and pick-up band in this bag.

Caring for Silk Fabrics

DRY CLEANING IS OFTEN RECOMMENDED for commercial silk garments. One reason is that the garment may be constructed of layers of fabric that include interfacing and linings, some of which may be damaged by water immersion. Another is that the manufacturer may be unsure of the wash-fastness of the dyes or the threads and findings used to sew and complete the garment.

However, as the spinner, dyer, weaver, knitter, and maker of the garment, you can control each of these factors. If you follow the guidelines outlined in this book—apply good-quality dyes properly, wash the yarn, wash and steam-press the fabric—you can be assured that washing and pressing will not harm the silk itself. You will only have to resort to dry cleaning if you choose interfacings, linings, or findings that will be damaged by water. Simple garments—those without fancy buttons or findings—can be safely handwashed. Silk garments need regular cleaning to remove perspiration salts, deodorants, perfumes, makeup, and any residue picked up during use and wear.

When I wash my handspun, handwoven, and handknitted silk garments, I fill a sink or tub with hot water and add a small amount of liquid soap. It's best to use a gentle, mild soap that's able to remove grease, such as hand-dishwashing soap. I try to use one that has no added dye or fragrance. Silk is damaged by most chemicals (except organic acids such as vinegar), and I don't want to risk adding any with the liquid soap.

I add the garment and let it soak for about an hour.

I then drain out or empty the soapy water, fill the tub with hot water, and rinse the garment. I repeat the rinsing process as necessary until the water runs clear.

For a final rinse, I add about 1/2 cup (120 milliliters) of distilled white vinegar to neutralize any alkaline or salts that may have been deposited on the garment.

I remove the garment from the water, squeeze out as much water as possible, then roll it in a towel to remove excess water. I then place the garment in the final spin cycle of my washing machine to remove any remaining water, followed by about 10 minutes in the dryer on high heat.

Then, I remove the still-damp garment from the dryer and press it with a hot iron to bring out the silky shine. Finer fabrics may only need a single pressing on each side; heavier fabrics might require several pressings.

When the fabric is sufficiently shiny, I hang it to finish drying.

CHAPTER FIVE:

Project Gallery

I encourage you to use your yarns. You might want to begin with small projects, bands, or braids, then move on to bags, scarves, and full garments. With use and experience, you'll find that handspun silk is suitable for many techniques and that it enhances any fabric you make.

Although I've been spinning, weaving, dyeing, and knitting with silk for more than thirty years, I still find magic in the luminous quality of the fiber and fabric, the feeling of almost impossible lightness and strength, and the glorious depth of color and shine. Silk may take a bit of getting used to, but your efforts will be rewarded with durable, long-wearing, and beautiful fabrics to wear and use.

The following pages are provided for inspiration and guidelines for your own adventures with handspun silk.

Fuchsia Warp-Painted Scarf

This scarf is the third in a series of scarves I wove to refine my technique for spinning bombyx from the fold to create fine, tight yarn. The first two scarves in the series marked the culmination of factors that allowed me to spin and weave the silk fabric I wanted to make—a tightly spun fine yarn, close-sett warp, and fine weft. To finish the scarf, I began with a vigorous wash, hot pressed it with an iron, then let it hang to dry. (You could also lay the scarf flat to dry.)

For the scarf shown here, I began with two bombyx bricks, one pre-dyed in a series of pinks and purples and the other white (which was later painted as a warp). I spun and plied the two colors separately on my wheel, wound them into warp chains, painted the white warp in colors that complemented the dyed fiber, and finished them with a bath of soapy water and a clear-water rinse.

The finished yarn wrapped at 40 wpi, so I sett the warp at 48 epi for a warp-dominant (but not warp-faced) structure. The weft is 40/3 mercerized cotton in purple. The cotton weft results in a crisp fabric that softens with use, and the color of the cotton coordinates with the dyed and painted silk.

The first two scarves in the series set me on my way to spinning the exceptional fabric shown here.

Teal Warp-Painted Scarf

For this scarf, the fourth of my early bombyx scarves, I also began with two bricks—one white and one that was already painted. I spun and plied the two colors separately on my wheel, wound them into warp chains, painted the white warp, and finished them with a bath of soapy water and a clear-water rinse.

As for the fuchsia scarf on page 102, I used a sett of 48 epi for a warp-dominant structure. This time, I chose a fine three-ply silk for the weft, which had about the same grist as the 40/3 cotton I had used previously. Either I'd become more adept at spinning silk and spun a finer warp yarn or the silk weft made more of a difference than I expected. This scarf has softened much more than the fuchsia scarf and was drapey to the point of being limp. Fabrics as soft as this scarf are perfect for next-to-the-skin garments, such as lingerie or fine blouses.

All silk fabrics soften with use and wear. But if they come off the loom soft and drapey, I find the fabric will be too limp after it's finished and subjected to even minor use. Both a closer sett and a weft with more body help prevent this degree of limpness.

The lessons I learned from the four scarves in this series, each with a different hand and drape, gave me the confidence to spin and weave fabric suitable for a jacket. Too bad I didn't realize the full impact and significance of weft choices when I started the jacket quest! Read on.

Scarf shown on page 99.

Kimono with Ikat & Painted Warp

For this kimono, the fifth in a series (others are shown on pages 80 and 81), I set out to make a jacket for everyday wear around town and at work (not too diaphanous or too fine a fabric). I selected colors that would coordinate with and liven up jeans or a denim skirt and that could span the seasons. Silk, which is both comfortable in warm weather and warm in cool weather, was the obvious choice. I just had to be sure not to make the fabric too heavy.

I spun and plied 22 ounces (624 grams) of white bombyx top in my usual way (two-plies at 40 wpi). I wound the finished yarn into an eight-yard (7.3-meter) warp, which I separated into four lots for different dye applications—immersion, ikat-resist, painted, and braid-resist. This gave me a variety of solid, banded, variegated, and mottled color effects. With each subsequent dye procedure, I made sure to incorporate colors that would coordinate with the ones already used.

For weft, I used commercial black 10/1 silk noil. Being a bit heavier than the wefts I used in previous kimonos, the "tooth" or texture in the raw silk helped to keep the fabric stable at seams and stress points. Despite the relatively large grist of the weft, silk is a lightweight fiber, so the hand of the fabric is pleasingly supple.

Patchwork Vest

I spun white bombyx top into a fine two-ply yarn to weave into fabric for a vest. I divided the yarn into separate warps that I painted to make two coordinating fabrics, each wrapped at 40 wpi and sett at 48 epi. I used a fine, shiny three-ply bombyx yarn for the weft in both.

Originally, I sewed the fabric into a vest that had tucked shoulder pleats and a wide front band closed with a button. After just a few wearings, though, the seams began to split—the weft was too slippery to hold the warps in place under the stress of the seams.

I gently took out the seams and applied a lightweight iron-on interfacing to the back of each piece. In addition to reinforcing the fabric, the interfacing added a stiffness that would be less attractive in the drapey style of the original vest. Instead, I cut strips of the two fabrics, sewed them together, and cut out new fronts, following a conventional vest pattern that's better suited for the stiffer fabric. I used commercial silk fabric for the back. The reinforced fabric has held up well, and there aren't any signs of the seams coming apart.

Although I was able to save the original fabric from complete failure, I prefer to learn from my mistakes and weave better fabric in the first place. Now, I routinely choose weft yarns that have a little texture or "tooth" and that results in sturdier fabric. My favorite is silk noil, either handspun or commercial, but other finely textured yarns such as wool, cotton, or cashmere work as well.

Red Vest

I wove the silk fabric for this vest as an experiment in combining yarns spun on spindles with yarns spun on a wheel. Having noticed that the amount of twist in a plied yarn can vary quite a bit in my warp yarns but have little effect in the appearance of plain-weave fabric, I'm quite relaxed as a spinner and don't get concerned about twist variation between skeins or warp chains.

While traveling, I spindle-spun and plied bombyx silk that had been pre-dyed a series of pale variegated colors. Back home, I wound the yarn into a 4-yard (3.6-meter) warp of 317 ends, which I knew wasn't wide enough for the vest I wanted. So, I wheel-spun and plied enough undyed bombyx until I had a total of 1,094 ends, which would produce a fabric that measured 22.8 inches (57.9 centimeters) wide when sett at 48 epi.

To unify the two batches of yarn, I overdyed the spindle-spun yarns deep red and painted all but ten ends of the wheel-spun yarn a series of reds and oranges. I dyed the remaining ten ends solid orange for accent stripes. I sleyed the spindle-spun yarns in wide stripes, separating them so that if they were to shrink differently than the wheel-spun yarns, I could segregate the two types of warp in the garment to highlight the differential shrinkage, or simply cut it off and not use it.

For weft, I chose a red commercial 30/2 angora-silk blend (7,000 yards [6,400 meters] per pound) for two reasons—it had enough "tooth" to prevent the silk warps from separating at the seams, and it was fine enough to allow flattering warpwise drape in the fabric.

I wove warp-dominant plain weave, finished the ends with zigzag stitching, and put

the fabric through a full wash cycle in my top-loading washer. I placed it in the dryer at full heat for a few minutes to eliminate some wrinkles, then pressed it with a very hot iron to bring out the shine and luster, and hung it over a fat pipe to dry completely.

Although the spindle-spun yarns appeared to be a bit finer in grist, more tightly twisted, and formed slightly thinner fabric than the wheel-spun yarns, I couldn't detect significant differences between the two in the surface of the finished fabric. I therefore cut the vest out of the full width of the cohesive fabric. I lined it with a coordinating printed rayon fabric.

Five Bags

The following five bags represent different construction techniques in small projects that use relatively little yarn and take little time to complete. They're useful first as samples, as you learn what grist and amount of twist you want to insert into your yarns, and later as bags, in and of themselves! I often recommend starting with small projects such as these so you can assess your yarn before committing to a larger piece of work.

Knitted Bag

Based on my experiments knitting with hand-spun silk (see page 88), I was pretty sure that a four-ply bombyx yarn would make a very nice knitted garment. However, before committing to a full garment, I wanted to try the hand of the fabric in a small bag.

After spinning and plying the yarn, I dyed it several colors for stranded-colorwork knitting.

I knitted the bag on size U.S. oo (1.75 mm) needles for a firm but supple fabric. I added a row of yarnover eyelets through which a kumihimo cord is drawn and finished the upper edge with firm crochet.

All in all, I think this experiment was a success. The fabric has nice drape that would translate well to a sweater, skirt, or shawl. The four-ply yarn provides the necessary body and strength, and the firm stitches bring out the luster and shine of the silk.

Crocheted Bag

First published in the Fall 2003 issue of *Spin·Off*, this small bag is an experiment in Shepherd's knitting and Bosnian crochet. I suspected that these techniques would be less abrasive to handspun silk than regular crochet because in each technique, the hook goes through only one loop to create a new stitch—the front loop for Shepherd's knitting, the back loop for Bosnian crochet.

Crochet yarns are typically twisted in the Z (clockwise) direction for the final twist. For this bag, I spun tussah silk in the Z direction, plied two strands in the S direction, and finally, plied two of the two-ply yarns in the Z direction to make a four-ply cabled yarn.

Cabled yarns are sturdy and hold up well through the process of making and in use. Cabling allows fine tight-twist silk yarns to be combined into yarns of larger grist for ease of working. It also secures the fibers in layers of twist, making the yarn particularly durable.

Pile Project Bag

This piece was many things before it became the bag you see here. The bottom section, worked in knotted pile, was initially intended to be a hat. I spun three-ply tussah for the warp, threaded the loom 23 inches (58.5 centimeters) wide. I wove the pile band, then the top section. I removed the fabric from the loom, wove in all the warp ends, washed the fabric, then sewed the five triangular shapes together to form the top of the hat, stitched the back seam, and trimmed and lined the hat with velvet.

To my dismay, the hat was too small for my head! For several years, I used it as a showpiece, sculpture, and cautionary tale, before I finally turned it into a bag.

To begin, I dipped the hat in a bath of discharge chemicals to remove some of the color, then I added a leather upper piece, velvet trimmings, buttons, beads, and a tablet-woven band made of handspun tussah silk.

My too-small hat is now just the right size for a project bag, but it (sadly) remains a cautionary tale.

Tablet-Woven Bag

For this bag, I spun two-ply tussah, dyed it, then tablet-wove a 6-foot (1.8-meter) band in the Egyptian Diagonals pattern. For the body of the bag, I sewed strips together side by side, then folded them at the tip of the front flap. I used the same yarn to make a round kumihimo band to trim the bag and added pennies to weight the flap when the bag is closed. Finally, I covered the back of the trim and edging with a small inkle band (woven with the same handspun silk), lined it with commercial silk fabric, and topped it off with another tablet-woven band for a handle.

This bag is an excellent example of how multiple techniques can be combined into a single unified piece.

Square-Bottom Spindle Bag

This spindle bag is another example of how a failed project can be transformed into a success. This fabric started out as a scarf made from two-ply yarn spun from tussah that I got from a variety of suppliers. Sometimes, this gamble works but, in this case, the yarn stretched differentially in the weaving, and the finished scarf was flimsy, floppy, and irregular along the selvedges.

To turn the disappointing fabric into a bag, I pieced and stitched it together and added a silk tablet-woven band that doubled as a handle and decoration. I lined the bag with commercial silk and trimmed it with commercial velvet. Now it's just right for carrying spindles.

Knitted Colors: Garter-Stitch Shawl

This shawl, modeled after a wool garter-stitch shawl of my grandmother's, is knitted from three-ply tussah yarn that I spindle-spun while traveling. I started with four colors of fiber—gold, orange, red, and wine. By spinning three-ply yarn, I was able to make gradual shifts from one color to the next. However, as I traveled and taught at shops and conferences, I found tussah dyed in an interim gold that I couldn't resist. Then I found just the right purple and blues. I'm sure I could have added colors endlessly, but there comes a time when a person just has to stop!

From my knitting experiments (see page 88), I was confident that a multiple-ply tussah yarn would have sufficient grist to keep the knitting process from becoming onerous or endless. And because I had used a similar yarn to weave a scarf, I knew that despite its apparent large size, the yarn would have sufficient drape and durability.

With size U.S. 3 (3.25 mm) needles, I cast on about a hundred stitches and worked on the scarf during my travels. I used the Russian method to join yarns "invisibly" and ensure that the ends would stay secure in the knitting even after trimming. Because silk doesn't felt or full like wool, cashmere, mohair, angora, or alpaca, there's a danger of the ends eventually working their way out of the knitting if they aren't suitably secured.

After binding off the stitches, I washed the shawl in hot soapy water, rinsed it, and spun out the moisture in the spin cycle of my washing machine. I then placed the shawl in the dryer for five minutes and hung it to dry. Finally, I trimmed the ends left from the Russian joins.

RUSSIAN JOIN

Bluefaced Leicester–Silk Triple Shawl

For this shawl, a blend of 75 percent Bluefaced Leicester and 25 percent bombyx silk dyed by Abstract Fibers and purchased at The Spinning Loft (see Resources), I started with dyed tops in two different colorways—one was nearly solid reds and purples, and the other had long color changes of reds, golds, and orange. Because I planned to spin the yarn while traveling, I decided to spin the two colorways separately and ply them together in a two-ply yarn with random color placement. This meant that I didn't have to pay attention to the color shifts as I spun or plied, which is always a good idea when spindle-spinning in random moments. After washing, the fiber yielded 700 yards (640 meters) of yarn.

I set out to make a shawl that could double as a pillow or blanket when I traveled by train or plane—so few comforts are offered to travelers these days that I like to carry my own. Because I wanted to use every inch (centimeter) of the yarn, I searched for a flexible pattern that would let me stop knitting whenever the yarn ran out.

I chose a random combination of stockinette, garter, and eyelet stitches in a three-panel design that would stay on my shoulders. Whenever a long stretch of color came up in the yarn, I switched from stockinette to garter stitch or inserted a row of eyelets. The color changes were thereby highlighted by changes in the surface structure.

Knitted Fall Leaves Shawl

I knitted this lace shawl for the Fall 2009 issue of *Spin·Off* and named it Fall Leaves as a nod to the color and stitch pattern. I spun white bombyx top into a two-ply yarn. After knitting the center panel the desired size, I picked up stitches around the four edges and knitted outward to add an edging around the entire perimeter. To ensure that the ends stayed secure, I used a Russian join (see page 119) when joining new balls of yarn.

When the knitting was complete, I dyed the shawl in a low-water immersion bath that transitioned from gold dye at one end to copper at the other. A mottled and variegated color effect took place in the center where the two colors met. Next, I painted the leaf motifs with a thickened dye solution and a small paintbrush. To set the dye in the painted areas, I wrapped the shawl in plastic and put it in a steam bath for thirty minutes. Finally, I rinsed the shawl, wrung out the water, and used a hot iron to block it before laying it flat to dry.

Knitted Flames Shawl

I knitted this three-panel shawl for the Winter 2011 issue of *SpinKnit*. I began with white bombyx top that I spun into two-ply yarn at about 7,500 yards (6,858 meters) per pound.

Inspired by the shape and colors of a gas flame, I designed a flame pattern that graduated from smaller motifs at the neckline to larger ones at the hem. I ended the shawl with a simple looped bind-off without adding a border or edging. I was able to knit the entire shawl out of a single skein of yarn so I didn't have to worry about joining yarn.

I washed the shawl in hot water with soap, then used thickened dye to paint the wet fabric in the colors I had imagined—a center blue flame, surrounded by golds and oranges (fire), and set off by the darkness of the purple background. I placed the shawl in a steam bath for thirty minutes to set the dye, then rinsed and pressed it dry with a hot iron.

Woven Wool– Silk–Cashmere Purple Shawl

I wove this shawl from a combination of two- and three-ply handspun yarns. With the intention of weaving with it, I spun the purple silk-cashmere blend in a fine two-ply yarn that wrapped at 24 wpi. Because the cashmere gave the yarn a fuzzy halo, I wanted to use a relatively open sett of 24 epi. But, as lovely as the purple was, I thought it needed more color, so I set it aside while I looked for fiber to add to it.

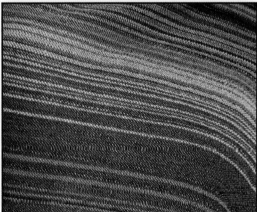

I spun a series of two-ply yarns on my wheel, all in the about the same grist as the silk-cashmere warp—merino-silk in a color called Ashes of Roses, another merino-silk in shades of red, and tussah-Corriedale-alpaca in soft beige. At the same, I happened to be spinning some beautiful, deep rich copper pygora on my spindle. One of the yarns, a soft rose merino-silk blend, I had spun into a three-ply yarn for knitting. The color looked great with all the rest of the yarns, and I knew that the three-ply wouldn't be a problem if I sleyed it as very narrow accent stripes across the entire width. All told, I had plenty of yarn to weave a long shawl. I measured a 4-yard (3.6 meter) warp for a weaving width of 27 inches (68.5 centimeters) and wove with a dark wine 48/3 merino from Colourmart for weft.

After weaving, I finished the ends with twisted fringe, then agitated the fabric in the washing machine for about 10 minutes, spun out the water, and placed it in the dryer on high heat for 5 minutes. To finish, I pressed it with a hot iron over a pressing cloth and hung it over a fat pipe to dry. The result is soft, warm, and substantial, despite the fine, lightweight fibers I began with.

"Carbonated Colors" Deb Menz

Carbonated Colors Wall Hanging

Silk has long been used for embroidery. Singles and very softly twisted plied yarns that flatten out in the work make a lustrous surface.

For this colorwork piece by Deb Menz, hand-spun singles silk in blended colors is embroidered in satin stitch to completely cover the background linen fabric. Deb graded the colors in the bubbles, outlined each unit, and worked a border of blue beads around the entire piece.

Glossary of Silk Terms

Fiber Preparation Terms

BATT. A carded fiber preparation of loosely aligned fibers. Batts are similar to laps, but batts contain fewer inclusions (chaff, noils, and foreign material) than laps.

BRICKS. Prepared from waste fibers from the reeling process, bricks are folded into compact rectangular shapes for storage and shipping. Bricks can be opened and spun as top, but because the fibers are in a larger bundle, they may require additional care in drafting.

COCOONS. Several types of cocoons are available for spinners to process. Bombyx, tussah, and eri cocoons can be dyed, made into hankies, or even reeled.

HANKIES. Also called mawata, hankies are attenuated cocoons that are stretched and dried and stored in layers. The fiber is suitable for spinning or used as wadding in clothing and quilts. Hankies may also come in the form of "caps" or "bells," which are simply cocoons attenuated over a bell-shaped form.

LAPS. Fiber from early stages of industrial processing, laps are similar to carded batts. The mostly aligned fibers are of varying lengths. Laps may contain more inclusions (chaff, noils, and foreign material) than batts.

NOILS. Noil silk fiber is short, full of small bits and inclusions, and spins into a textured yarn with little luster. Noil silk yarns have the strength, drape, and durability of silk, but the finished yarns more closely resemble cotton in appearance.

TOP. The waste fibers from silk reeling are processed into an aligned preparation of similar-length fibers suitable for spinning by hand or machine. Top is available as a long ribbon of unspun fiber, usually about 1" (2.5 cm) in diameter.

Reeled Silk Terms

REELING. The task of unwinding cocoons onto a frame. Cocoons are stifled (the worm is killed) and placed into pots of very warm water with a small amount of alkaline to soften the sericin. Several cocoons are unwound at one time into one thread; the number of cocoons determines the size of the thread being wound. As each cocoon is finished and drops out of the bundle, a new one is inserted to replace it, which keeps the diameter of the winding yarn uniform.

THROWING. Once the cocoons have been reeled into a continuous thread, twist is added to the length of the thread in a process called throwing (similar to spinning, twist is added to the filament, but there is no drafting). The number of strands in the yarn is preset in the reeling process.

DOUBLING. Two yarns which have been thrown are twisted together in the reverse direction to added strength and diameter to the forming yarn (similar to plying).

DEGUMMING. The process of removing sericin from silk fibers. There are several points at which sericin can be removed: in the fiber before processing; in the yarn after reeling or spinning but before dyeing; or in the fabric after weaving.

DENIER. An indicator of the density of a silk yarn. One denier is said to be the weight of one full strand of silk (9,000 yards), which is one gram. Two-denier silk would weigh two grams per 9,000 yards. The lower the number, the finer the silk yarn.

TRAM SILK. A reeled yarn that has not been twisted (thrown) at all or only very slightly so. It has shiny filaments and is used as weft in weaving, as well as for embroidery, where its luster predominates.

ORGANZINE. A reeled yarn that has been twisted (thrown) and plied (doubled).

Silk Fabric Terms

Silk fabrics can be described by weave structure, weight, and customary fabric name. A few of the terms you might encounter are listed here.

BROCADE. A woven silk, decorated with a surface design of yarn separate from the structure of the cloth. If the brocade design is removed, a plain-weave fabric will remain. There are weft brocade patterns and, less commonly, warp brocade patterns.

CHARMEUSE. A satin-weave fabric, prized for its drape and sheen. Usually used in lingerie and evening clothing.

CHIFFON. A lightweight fabric woven from high-twist yarns into a fine and sheer web. Chiffon is often used for sheer clothing, as an over layer for silk evening garments, and for lingerie. The fabric has stretch and recovery qualities because of the performance of the high-twist yarns.

CRÊPE DE CHINE. In this crepe-weave fabric, the matte surface reflects less light than other silk fabrics. It drapes well and wrinkles less than flat weaves. The weft yarn in this fabric is tightly twisted, giving it the ability to stretch and recover.

DOUPPIONI. A fabric with a textured surface, woven from cocoons joined during the process of spinning by the silkworms, called double cocoons. The area where the cocoons are joined makes a thicker spot in the yarn, giving douppioni silk its characteristics uneven surface texture. It's a firm fabric, suitable for tailored garments and for home decorating fabric.

EMBOSSED. A fabric that has been pressed with heat and pressure, resulting in a design or pattern, so that the surface has been altered. See watermarked.

HABOTAI. A lightweight and smooth plain-weave silk fabric, used often for linings. It's sold by weight or by momme.

MOMME (MM). A term used to describe the thickness of a silk fabric: the finer the fabric, the lower the number. The number refers to the weight in pounds of a 45-inch-wide fabric 100 yards long. For example, 45 inches × 100 yards of an 8 mm fabric would weigh 8 pounds (3.6 kilograms).

SILK NOIL. Sometimes called raw silk, this fabric has small neps or noils embedded in the yarn, giving it a rustic texture and surface. Noil silk is usually off-white and has a more casual look than fine silk fabrics. It resists wrinkles and packs well.

SATIN. A weave structure used for silk fabrics, one side of which has the warps held in close proximity, while the other side shows more of the weft. Charmeuse is a satin-weave silk fabric.

TAFFETA. A weftwise rib weave woven with a heavier weft over a fine and closely sett warp, making a strong and durable fabric used in tailored fashions and for home decorating.

VELVET. A pile fabric, with a ground warp and a separate pile warp. The pile warp is pulled forward into loops on the surface of the fabric and held in place by the interweaving of the ground warp and weft. The loops are cut during the finishing process; they may be sculpted in the cutting process to give depth and dimension to a design.

WATERMARKED. Wet silk fabric that has been run through a series of rollers that create an impression into the surface of the fabric. Sometimes called moiré or calendaring, the technique makes a surface impression that can be lost if the fabric is wetted.

WEIGHTED. Fabric to which mineral salts have been added to give it extra thickness, body, and weight. These salts are corrosive to the fibers and will cause cracking and disintegration of the fibers. Weighted silks are not durable over the long term.

Resources

Most of the resources I use for fiber are to be found at festivals and conferences. Their websites list many of their products, and I continue to buy online when there's no conference coming up. Support your local fiber suppliers, and they will continue to support us!

Silk and silk blends, equipment, and yarns for the products in this book were purchased from the following suppliers.

Abstract Fibers
abstractfiber.com

Acme Fibres (Hound Design Spindles)
acmefibres.com

Batt Music
etsy.com/shop/battmusic

Carin Engen
etsy.com/shop/carinengenfiberarts

Carolina Homespun
carolinahomespun.com

Cloverleaf Farms Hand Dyed Fiber (Joan Berner)
joanberner.com

ColourMart
colourmart.com/us

Enting Fibercraft Dyed Batts
etsy.com/shop/entingfibercraft

Fiber Optic
kimberbaldwindesigns.com

Fleecepickers Fiber and Yarn
fleecepickers.com

Freyalyn's Fibers
etsy.com/shop/freyalyn

Golding Spindles
goldingfibertools.com

Gnomespun Yarn
gnomespunyarn.com

Greensleeves Spindles
greensleevesspindles.com

IST Crafts (spindles)
thewoodemporium.co.uk

Lambspun of Colorado
lambspun.com

Lendrum Spinning Wheels
lendrum.ca

Lucky Cat Craft
etsy.com/shop/luckycatcraft

Luscious Luxury Dyed Fibers
www3.telus.net/rfws/lusciousluxury

Lunatic Fringe Yarns
lunaticfringeyarns.com

Mad Angel Creations
etsy.com/shop/madangelcreations

Opulent Fibers
opulentfibers.com

Portland Fibers
portlandfibergallery.com

Treenway Silks
treenwaysilks.com

Rainbow Farms Pygora
rfpygora.com

Redfish Dyeworks
redfishdyeworks.com

Schacht Spindle
company schachtspindle.com

Shuttles, Spindles and Skeins
shuttlesspindlesandskeins.com

Spinning Loft
thespinningloft.com

Spinning Forth (Ruth MacGregor)
spinningforth.com

Spirit Trail Fiberworks
spirit-trail.net

Spunky Eclectic
spunkyeclectic.com

Stringtopia (Abby Franquemont)
stringtopia.net/shop

Weaver Creek Fibers
weavercreekfibers.com

Yarn Chef
etsy.com/shop/yarnchef

Bibliography

Carboni, Dr. Paolo. *Silk*. London: Chapman and Hall, 1952.

Casey, Maggie. *Start Spinning*. Loveland, Colorado: Interweave, 2009.

Datta, Rajat, and Mahesh Nanavaty. *Global Silk Industry*. Boca Raton, Florida: Universal Publishers, 2005.

Feltwell, Dr. John. *The Story of Silk*. New York: St. Martin's Press, 1990.

Hochberg, Bette. *Fiber Facts*. Self published, 1981.

———. *Handspinner's Handbook*. Self published, 1976.

———. *Spin Span Spun*. Self published, 1979.

Joseph, Marjory L. *Essentials of Textiles*. Austin, Texas: Holt, Rinehart and Winston, 1984.

Kolander, Cheryl. *A Silkworker's Notebook*. Loveland, Colorado: Interweave, 1985.

Lamb, Sara. *Spin To Weave*. Loveland, Colorado: Interweave, 2013.

Lowry, Priscilla. *The Secrets of Silk: Myths and Legends*. London: St. John's Press, 2003.

———. *The Secrets of Silk: Textiles to Fashion*. London: St. John's Press, 2003.

MacGregor, Rugh. *Learn to Spin Silk*. Self published: www.spinningforth.com.

Peigler, Richard. *Wild Silks of the World. Spin·Off* magazine Winter 1999.

Schoeser, Mary. *Silk*. New Haven, Connecticut: Yale University Press, 2007.

Scott, Phillipa. *The Book of Silk*. London: Thames and Hudson, 1993.

Selk, Karen. *Journeys in the Wild Silk Jumgles of India. Spin·Off* magazine Spring 2000.

Spin·Off magazine Fall 2009. Interweave, 2009.

Spin·Off magazine. Fall 2003. Interweave, 2003.

Spring, Chris, and Julie Hudson. *Silk in Africa*. London: British Museum Press, 2002.

Varribm A. et al. *Ciba Review #11*, July, 1938.

Wyatt, James, and Anne Wardwell. *When Silk Was Gold*. New York: Harry Abrams, 1997.

Although it's not a book, I used the following website for my research on wild silks:

www.cdfd.org.in/wildsilkbase/home.php
Arunkumar KP, Tomar A, Daimon T, Shimada T and Nagaraju J (2008) WildSilkbase: An EST database of wild silkmoths. BMC Genomics 9:338.

Plans for a PVC Yarn Blocker

Materials

You will need 16 feet (4.9 m) of ¾" (2 cm) PVC pipe cut into the following lengths:

- Six 10" (25.5 cm) lengths *for blocking surface*

- Fourteen 6" (15 cm) lengths *for arms, handle, and short sides of base*

- Two 16" (40.5 cm) lengths *for long sides of base*

- Two 3" (7.5 cm) lengths *for axles*

You will also need the following parts:

- Fourteen 90° elbow-joints

- Two T-joints

- Two end-caps

- Two slip-joints (available as *furniture-grade PVC part*)

- Two 5-way connectors (available *as furniture-grade PVC part*)

Assembly

BASE: Assemble the base with two 16" (40.5 cm) lengths, four 6" (15 cm) lengths, four elbow-joints, and two T-joints. Glue all joins with PVC glue.

Glue one 10" (25.5 cm) length into each of two T-joints, top each with a slip-joint, then glue all in place, orienting the slip-joint so that the opening faces the center of the blocker.

AXLE: Insert a 3" (7.5 cm) length into each slip-joint for the axle but do not glue—the blocker must turn freely on this axle.

Glue an end-cap to the outside end of one 3" (7.5 cm) length piece, making sure the slip-joint turns freely.

HANDLE: Attach one elbow-joint to the outside end of the other 3" (7.5 cm) length, attach one 6" (15 cm) length to the other end of the elbow-joint, then attach another elbow-joint to the open end. Glue in place.

Attach another 6" (15 cm) length to the open elbow-joint and finish off with an end-cap. Glue in place, making sure that the axle turns freely.

REEL: Attach four 6" (15 cm) lengths to the four arms of each 5-way connector. Glue in place.

Glue an elbow-joint to the end of each arm.

Slip the 5-way connectors onto the 3" (7.5 cm) axles. Carefully glue in place, being careful that no glue gets into the slip-joint and that the axle turns freely.

Attach four 10" (25.5 cm) lengths between the elbows to connect the arms. Glue in place.

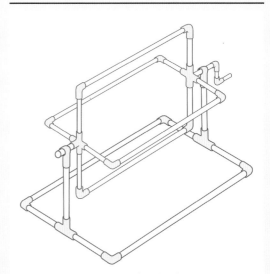

Simple tools can be made from hardware store parts.

Index

Enjoy an *inspiring collection* of *spinning wisdom* with these technique–filled books from Interweave.

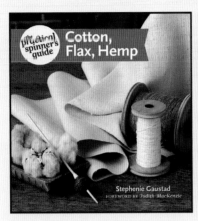

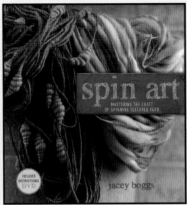

The Practical Spinner's Guide: *Cotton, Flax, Hemp*
Stephanie Gaustad
ISBN 978-1-59668-669-4
$26.99

Spin Art
Mastering the Craft of Spinning Textured Yarn
Jacey Boggs
ISBN 978-1-59668-362-4
$26.95

Start Spinning
Everything You Need to Know to Make Great Yarn
Maggie Casey
ISBN 978-1-59668-065-4
$21.95

Available at your favorite retailer or

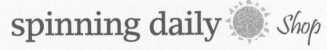

shop.spinningdaily.com

The magazine that highlights the vibrant and diverse spinning community and explores the intricacies of the craft. *Spinoffmagazine.com*

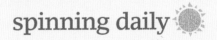

Join the online community just for spinners! You'll get a free eNewsletter, free patterns, pattern store, blogs, event updates, galleries, tips and techniques, and much more! Sign up at *Spinningdaily.com*